Dr. Bob and
Bill W. Speak:
AA's Cofounders
Tell Their Stories

Michael Fitzpatrick

Dr. Bob and Bill W. Speak: AA's Cofounders Tell Their Stories

 Hazelden
Publishing

Hazelden Publishing
Center City, Minnesota 55012
hazelden.org/bookstore

Library of Congress Cataloging-in-Publication Data

Fitzpatrick, Michael, 1959–
    Dr. Bob and Bill W. speak : AA's cofounders tell their stories / Michael
Fitzpatrick.
        p. cm.
    ISBN 978-1-61649-415-5 (softcover) -- ISBN 978-1-61649-451-3 (e-book)
1. Alcoholics Anonymous--History. 2. W., Bill 3. Smith, Robert Holbrook, 1879-
1950. 4. Alcoholics--Rehabilitation. I. Title.
    HV5278.A78F58 2012
    362.29'286--dc23
                        2012027682

In chapter 4, Earl's story is excerpted from "He Sold Himself Short" in
Alcoholics Anonymous, 4th ed. (New York: Alcoholics Anonymous World
Services, 2001), pp. 262–263. The Twelve Traditions and brief excerpts from
Alcoholics Anonymous are reprinted with permission of Alcoholics Anonymous
World Services, Inc. ("AAWS"). Permission to reprint brief excerpts from A.A.
material does not mean that AAWS has reviewed or approved the contents of
this publication, or that AAWS necessarily agrees with the views expressed
herein. A.A. is a program of recovery from alcoholism *only* — use of its material in connection with programs and activities which are patterned after A.A.,
but which address other problems, or in any other non-A.A. context, does not
imply otherwise.

Images of letters in appendix B courtesy Stepping Stones Foundation Archives
Center, Stepping Stones, the historic home of Bill and Lois Wilson, Katonah, NY.

Editor's note
The names, details, and circumstances may have been changed to protect the
privacy of those mentioned in this publication.
    Alcoholics Anonymous, AA, the Big Book, the *Grapevine*, and *AA Grapevine*
are registered trademarks of Alcoholics Anonymous World Services, Inc.

22 21 20 19   4 5 6 7 8

Cover design by David Spohn
Interior design and typesetting by David J. Farr, ImageSmythe

Legacy 12

Bringing AA and Twelve Step History Alive

Hazelden's *Legacy 12* publishing initiative enriches people's
recovery with dynamic multimedia works
that use rare original-source documents to bring Alcoholics
Anonymous and Twelve Step history alive.

To those who have chosen to follow Dr. Bob and Bill W.

contents

Appendices

guide to the audio cd

The CD included with this book offers highlights from archival recordings of AA's cofounders—the two men known as Bill W. and Dr. Bob—and the voices of others who knew them well. Dozens of hours of recordings were excerpted, transcribed, and adapted for inclusion in the book. While the CD contains some of this audio, it does not parallel the book exactly and is not intended as a "listen-along" disc. Instead, it serves as a collection of accounts and reflections that, together, create a portrait of these two visionaries.

In the pages of this book, this icon 🎧 shows that a related audio selection can be found on the disk. The number on the icon matches the track number.

CD Tracks
Total running time: approx. 80 minutes

1. Bill W. recalls stories from his childhood, speaking at the Texas State AA Convention in Fort Worth, June 1954. (7:51)

2. Bill W.'s sponsor, Ebby T., shares several stories from his own life before he joined the Oxford Group, speak-

ing at an AA meeting in Great Bend, Kansas, February 21, 1961. (4:11)

3. Bill W. recounts Ebby's visit with him in November 1934 and his own spiritual experience shortly thereafter, speaking in Chicago, February 1951. (5:11)

4. Bill W. recalls "preaching" to other alcoholics in the months before he met Dr. Bob, speaking on July 14, 1951. (3:55)

5. On the twentieth anniversary of his own sobriety, November 9, 1954, Bill W. speaks on personal transformation and William James's book The Varieties of Religious Experience. (3:25)

6. In Detroit in 1948, Dr. Bob recounts his first meeting with Bill W. on May 12, 1935—the meeting that would give rise to Alcoholics Anonymous. (4:23)

7. In the same speech, Dr. Bob talks about the importance of "the spirit of service." (3:16)

8. Bill W. tells about his first meeting with Dr. Bob, speaking in Akron on Founders Day, June 1954. (4:35)

9. Clarence S., the founder of AA in Cleveland, recounts his experience with Dr. Bob and other AA pioneers while he was hospitalized in Akron City Hospital. Clarence spoke at Lake Brownwood, Texas, September 15, 1962. (6:11)

10. On June 20, 1965, Bill W. describes the influence of St. Francis on him as he wrote the book Alcoholics Anonymous some thirty years earlier. (3:14)

11. At a 1951 speech in San Francisco, Bill W. notes the powerful early example of Sister Ignatia, asking, "Who says AA has only two founders?" (2:24)

12. Sister Ignatia recalls Dr. Bob and Anne S., speaking at AA's International Convention, July 3, 1960. (2:59)

13. "Love and service" are the essence of AA, says Dr. Bob in his farewell talk at the First International Convention of AA in Cleveland, July 1950. (2:09)

14. In this 1948 speech in Detroit, Dr. Bob reflects on the importance of maintaining his sobriety. (5:51)

15. Recalling his early days on Clinton Street in New York with his wife, Lois, Bill speaks at the annual Manhattan Group Christmas party, 1955. (3:00)

16. At the same meeting, Bill discusses the writing of the Twelve Steps. (1:37)

17. "The sun never sets upon this fellowship," remarks Bill W. in a speech titled "Our Responsibility to AA's Future" at AA's International Convention in Toronto, July 1965. (3:41)

18. In the same speech, Bill W. reminds his audience that AA should be inclusive. (3:05)

19. Bill W. closes by describing the board of trustees' confidence in the evolving organization. (3:22)

20. Bill W. and Mike Wallace both repeat the Serenity Prayer at the end of a 1956 radio interview. (0:53)

21. In this June 1947 exchange of wire recordings between Dr. Bob and Bill W., Bill closes by playing a German folk tune on his violin. (4:42)

Guide to the Audio CD

Introduction

CERTAIN QUESTIONS CAME UP several times during discussions about the writing of *Dr. Bob and Bill W. Speak*: "What's going to be different about this book?" or "What is there to say that hasn't already been discussed in other books?"

I've had more than twenty years of sales experience. I know that when the same question keeps being asked, it needs to be answered, or forget about getting the sale! The answer is Yes, I will present material throughout this book that has not been made readily available or published in other books. I will share the AA story, as much as possible, by using the actual words of the cofounders, Dr. Bob and Bill W., from their talks and letters.

The process of doing this is hampered a bit by the fact that Dr. Bob died in 1950 and to date there are only four known recordings containing his voice, and two of those are less than five minutes in length. Because of this, I will include some information taken from recordings and other sources, including AA members, "sponsees," and friends who knew the cofounders.

I have spent a considerable amount of time studying and researching Alcoholics Anonymous, and I've noticed that the history of AA seems to have many conflicting stories, depending on the particular version you hear. It also seems that just about all of these versions are true to some extent or at least insofar as the person who communicated the story believed it to be true; in other words, it's a matter of perception.

I have many friends in both AA and Al-Anon. Two of my dearest friends, Howard and Pat P. of Gilbert, Arizona, have been members of their respective fellowships for forty years. Howard shared the following story with me, which illustrates how perceptions can differ and still have their own truth.

> Our culture teaches us that it is important to be right, in large part, in order to do the right things. When I was near my third year of sobriety, and my wife in her third year of Al-Anon, we were going through a rather long period of general disagreement about many things: budgets, household and personal expenses, how to raise our children, and much more. Our lives had become kind of an ongoing battle about many issues.
>
> One day we were angrily arguing about some issue, I don't remember what, but I remember that on my way home from work I was busy going over my arguments. When I got home and into the house, Pat smiled and said, "Hello, honey. I talked to Ruth [her Al-Anon sponsor] about our issue today, and she said that you were right."
>
> "Good for Ruth," I thought. "I have always thought she had a great head on her shoulders."
>
> But before I could really respond, Pat added, "But she said that I was right too."
>
> "Okay," I guardedly replied. "Just what did Ruth say?"
>
> "She said that she didn't think our issue was really worth fighting over; and she didn't think we were really fighting over the issue. She said she thought we were fighting over who was going to be right. Then she said that she thought we were both right."
>
> That stymied me for a moment and I responded, "And?"
>
> "And," Pat continued, still smiling, "she said that we simply had different points of view, and from both of our points of view, we were both right. Ruth then took a dollar bill out of her purse

and held it in front of me with me looking at the front side of the bill and with her looking at the other side.

"Now," she told me, "if you describe exactly what you see on your side of this dollar bill, and then I describe exactly what I see on my side of the same dollar bill, it will sound like we are describing two different things. But we know that we are simply looking at the same dollar bill from different points of view."

"Well I'll be," I told Pat. "She is absolutely right about that." And, as it turned out, Ruth's point of view about our fighting turned out to be one of the most effective solutions to our disagreements that we could have had.[1]

As you read the following chapters, keep in mind that what you read may not be the same version of the story that you've heard elsewhere. For example, in the second chapter, you will find that Ebby's version of the famous "kitchen table" exchange differs somewhat from Bill's description in the Big Book.

Which version is accurate? Some claim that Ebby's story must be true, considering he was sober while Bill was drunk. Others argue that Ebby told the story many years later, after he had had several severe relapses. His chronic alcoholism had affected his brain so that he was simply mistaken and his recall of the situation from twenty-five years earlier was more illusion than reality.

Regardless of which side you stand on, we are faced with two very different recollections of the same event. There seem to be many instances of this type of discrepancy throughout AA history. One friend recently said, "What do you expect? We're talking about alcoholics."

This book does not set out to answer any questions or to "set right" any previous versions of AA history. Perhaps allowing the founders to tell "what happened" in their own words is the best way. We can then consider the material and make our own decisions based on our ability to interpret their messages.

Bill W.'s sobriety began after Ebby T.'s visit to him at his home on Clinton Street in Brooklyn, New York. I've decided to begin with Ebby's story. Following that, you will read about Bill's spiritual experience and then about the famous meeting between Bill W. and Dr. Bob on Mother's Day in 1935 in Akron, Ohio, which led to the founding of Alcoholics Anonymous. The remainder of the book will highlight many events and circumstances that occurred within the AA movement during the lives of the cofounders, Dr. Bob S. and Bill W., told as much as possible in their own words taken from speeches archived in my audio library, Recovery Speakers Research Center, and from their correspondence, made available by Stepping Stones, the former home of Bill and Lois Wilson that is now a museum housing AA historical archives.

Ever since I obtained my audio library (read more about this library on page 211), I knew that I wanted not only wanted to preserve the audio history of AA and Al-Anon, but also to determine how to best make it available to others. This, of course, remains an ongoing concern, and as time passes new opportunities are presented.

I am most grateful to the directors and staff at Hazelden Publishing for their support and encouragement in allowing me the privilege of making available selected materials in book form.

Prologue

BEFORE WE GET INTO THE STORIES OF AA'S FOUNDATIONS, let's start with some of Bill's stories of his early life and the events leading up to his meeting the man known as Ebby T.

The following account is excerpted from a speech Bill W. gave in Dallas, Texas, in June 1951.

1

I was raised in a little Vermont town of about fifty inhabitants. My old grand-pappy brought me up. I suppose you consider those folks in Vermont the most errant of Yankees. But I must observe that even the governor of Texas has made me an honorary citizen of this state. Anyhow my grand-pappy brought me up and he brought me up for this reason — that my mother and father had been divorced. Well, back in those days there was as much or more stigma on divorce in a small Yankee town as there was on being the town drunk, almost.

So at ten years of age I heard the gossip of the neighbors. I began to feel different. I began to feel that I didn't belong. Then, too, I was awkward, physically awkward, pretty homely, just like I am now. Except then I cared much and now I don't care a damn. I remember being very cast down as a kid, from ten to twelve. And then this fierce desire to win out over these handicaps took possession of me. A desire so fierce that it turned into what the medics call a neurosis — a ten-dollar word which means, folks, a person who is mentally sane but emotionally crazy as I shall presently show you.

So I developed a tremendous drive to distinguish myself, to be somebody that far transcended normal ambition. And the neighbors — I remember one of my old friends, barefoot Rose. She used to say, point at me, and she'd say, "That Willy's got a lot of persistence. He's going a long way that boy." She couldn't guess how far down. My grandfather, seeing this trait in me, wanted to encourage it. So he was always proposing the impossible.

One day he came in and said, "Will, I've been reading a book about Australia. The natives have got a weapon down there they call a boomerang and when they throw it, if it misses its mark, it returns to the caster. And Will," said he in a challenging way, "nobody but an Australian can make and throw a boomerang." Well, I said what was probably the childish equivalent of, "The hell you say, Grand-pappy!"

Immediately I'm in a public library — all the books about Australia out. I'm trying to learn all about boomerangs, out in the old shop with the lantern at night whittling boomerangs. Well, you say, any kid would have done that. Yes, that's true. But no kid would have done that six solid months to the exclusion of everything else — boomerangs, boomerangs, boomerangs. No schoolwork done, no wood box filled, no nothing. I had to be the first, mark this, the number one white man to make and throw a boomerang, age eleven.

Finally I cut the head out of my bed because it had just the right piece of wood to make a boomerang out of. And at the end of six months I could make and throw a boomerang and I called Grand-pappy out to see, cast one around the churchyard; it circled it, slid back down, and Grand-pappy ducked or it would have cut his poor old head off. Well, that was the boomerang business. Interest all evaporates then in boomerangs — I'd done it!

Next thing we know Grand-pappy says, "Well, Will, I don't think you got much ear for music." Well he was stating a fact; I'd not taken the slightest interest ever. But he said, "Uncle Clarence's fiddle is up there in the trunk. You know he died of TB out there in Denver. When he was a boy your Uncle Clarence could, well, he could play the fiddle, he could play the Jew's harp, he could play the harmonica. "But Willy," he said, "I don't think you got any ear for music."

So, right up to that trunk, out with the fiddle, one string on it. Put a chip under it for a bridge and I start sawing on that fiddle — now to be what? The first violin of the high school orchestra, I'm going to be. Lessons? No, I'll learn myself. Get some wire strings at the grocery store and I fiddle, fiddle, fiddle, until I drove 'em just nuts. And I did become the leader of the high school orchestra and an awful band it was.

I arrived now at boarding school. I'm awkward, so because I'm awkward I got to be an athlete. A boy throws a ball. I don't get my hands up to catch it. It hits me in the head. I'm knocked down. Well, I wasn't physically hurt but how bitter I was when I saw those kids stand in a circle around me and laugh. And I got up and shook my fist and I said, "I'll be captain of your damn ball team." Number one, number one, well I was! Got a crooked arm here from throwing rocks so much at telephone poles.

Then something happens that gives you the other side of this coin. The other side of this implacable urge — going way beyond any normal ambition to excel, to dominate, to be famous. See the other side of this coin.

I was awkward, as I said. I had terrible inferiority about the gals; none did pay much attention to me until I began to get along in athletics. Finally the minister's daughter, well she sort of took me up. You know women do it that way. So now you see in boarding school I'm deliriously happy. I'm a success; I'm the number one fellow all over the place. In that period I think people would have called me extremely egotistical. But actually, deep down I was driven by this perpetual fear, inferiority, and still haunted by the feeling that I didn't quite belong. But if I couldn't belong I would rule.

So now the picture is complete. I'm in love for the first time. One morning the principal came into the chapel with a very long face and he said, "I don't know how to tell you the terrible news that Bertha Banford [the minister's daughter] died last night — suddenly stricken." I still tremble as I remember that. For me, the end of the world had come. I fell into a deep depression; it lasted for months. It lasted for years.

Was there anything normal about that? No! If I'd been an average kid, oh I would have felt very badly, but I would have brushed away the tears and ninety days later I would have had my arms around another one; wouldn't I? But not me, now I'm depressed. I can only saw on that fiddle. No athletics, no interest in anything. I don't graduate from school.

Three years later the wonderful woman who was to see me almost to hell and back came into my life and tenderly raised me up out of the bog I was in. Up to this time, not a drink of liquor. World War breaks out. I'm in a military school now. People think I need the discipline. I guess they were right. Well, in Vermont it's a tradition that everybody bears arms so I'm presently off to the war as a young officer.

Well, and down in New Bedford, a cotton town, and the society people take us up down there, us young officers. Well, as I say, I came from a small town of about fifty houses — back doorstep one of the conveniences, you know. I felt, again, this terrible sense of being ill at ease — I didn't belong — this terrible awkwardness, the shyness, this terrible inferiority.

Then somebody handed me my first drink. I'd refrained hitherto because there was a tradition in my family that most of the Wilsons were drunks and I'd better not start it. But this time, under these conditions, I was given a cocktail. How well I remember; it was a Bronx, and boy I liked it.[2] Another, another, and then a miracle seemed to happen. A strange barrier which had stood between me and other people seemed to fall. For the first time I felt that I belonged. People drew near to me, I drew near to them. There was communication of a kind that I'd never had. I have discovered the elixir of life.

Now all the drunks here really know what I'm talking about. A little aside to our friends; you see, at once, liquor meant more to me. Even then, right then, I was not using a drink for relaxation; I commenced to use it to solve my life's problem. And the problem at that moment was my fear and inferiority of all these strange and, I supposed, very superior people. So that started it; I guess I got drunk that very night. I remember being terribly drunk in the officer's club there in New Bedford and having to be carried home.

Then came the World War and going abroad. I'm sitting in the bottom of the hold on guard during the night so that if a torpedo hit, the men wouldn't panic: I had orders to shoot them. All of sudden there was a terrible crash. I thought we were hit and up to this moment I'd felt I was a coward, that I'd let my state down because I'd joined the artillery instead of the aviation. And yet feeling that we were gone, I did draw my gun, stopped the panic, and a great exultation seized me.

After that the war was kind of fun, and it was powered all through by liquor. Well then I found that I got along well with the men. All the time in this period I was drinking to dream greater dreams of power, of ambition.

When I got home, I was like all the vets coming home now; I had to start at the bottom. I'm no longer an officer; I'm clerk in the New York Central Railroad. They toss me out of that because I can't keep books. I'm a socialist; I study law, nights, and begin to say to the people in the great city, "I'll show you."

While I was taking a law course, I became an investigator for a surety company that took me into Wall Street. That was a shortcut to fame; meanwhile, the drinking [was] building up and up and up. Well, in those days it was a "good man's fault," but my poor wife, Lois, knew it to be something much more than that — as I came home having crawled under a subway gate because I didn't have a nickel, [after] being rolled. That sort of thing had begun to happen.

Oh yes we were living in a very swell apartment, but she knew that I had something more than just a habit. Alcoholism had already laid a hold of me. Well, more money came in than was good for me. Then came the Crash; it was all swept away.

I remember the contempt with which I regarded people who were committing suicide by jumping from the towers of high finance. And I remember beating on my chest and said, "I have done this once, I can do it again." And again, the old fierce desire to succeed seized me. This I will do; the drinking went up and up, to dream more and more.

But now I begin to run over onto the other side of the road. When I signed that contract, I really meant it. And my new friend said, "Bill, with this new prospect surely you're not going to drink this up. But please sign a contract that if you take one drink your contract will be over." I knew this to be the greatest financial opportunity I might ever have. I believed I could do it. I did not yet realize that I was already possessed of an obsession that condemned me to drink against my will — against my desires, against my home, against all my interests. An obsession that condemned me to go on drinking and an increasing physical sensitivity that guaranteed that one day I would go mad or die.

Inside of three months I was drunk again. I was with some people and they had some applejack, "Jersey Lightning" they called it. I refused it several times with great ease and then with equal ease I suddenly said to myself, "Well, you never had any Jersey Lightning, Bill, never, never in all your drinkin'. One little bowl of Jersey Lightning won't hurt you." Three days later I'm dead drunk in the hotel; my contract was at an end; again the bottom fell out.

My progress down was so fast that soon the doctors were saying, "Well, not much hope." One cure after another, and finally on a summer's day in 1934 a doctor who was destined to play a great part in our society was obliged to tell Lois, "I'm afraid he's going to be like all the rest. Nearly all the rest had passed my way."

"What do you mean, Doctor?" said she. "How bad is this?"

"Well," he said, "I thought that Bill was one of those people I could reeducate. He has been a man of immense willpower. I thought if he better understood the malady, well, maybe he'd be one of the few."

Dr. Bob and Bill W. Speak

She said, "Doctor, but what do you mean?"

"Well," he said, "I hate to tell you this, but, Mrs. Wilson, if you expect him to live long or to stay sane, I think you will have to lock him up." Condemned by an obsession to go on drinking; condemned by a physical sensitivity to go mad or die. That was the dilemma and I hit bottom and my god of science, for I worshiped science having had an engineering training, having been brought up with one of those dandy modern educations which had declared that man was god and could do anything, but here now was my god of science saying that I'm hopeless, hopeless. At last I got the full import of that. Fear possessed me. I left that place.

By dint of the greatest vigilance I avoided liquor; I stayed sober for several months, something unheard of for me. I even went to the Street and made a few dollars. I felt quite alright, perfectly well. Lois [was] still at work. And then again suddenly on Armistice Day 1934 I'm again caught in the toils. The obsession grabbed me — one drink wouldn't hurt me. I'm dead drunk, wander around all day and all night coming home dragging a golf bag with a great cut on my head.

Lois, going to work, finds me in the morning. Well, November 11th, 1934, marked the beginning of my last debauch. I went on drinking steadily — a quart of bathtub a day, sometimes two or three. "Bathtub," my friend, means a species of gin made in Prohibition time.

One afternoon the telephone rang. An old schoolmate was on the other end of the wire. I hadn't seen him for years. I had never known of his being in New York City sober, and long since I'd recognized that he was one like me caught in this fatal trap. But here he was in New York, sober.[3]

The case can be made that the first AA meeting took place at Bill W.'s kitchen table that night in November 1934 when his old schoolmate and drinking buddy Ebby T. showed up sober and exclaimed, "I've got religion!" We'll now turn to Ebby's version of the story in his own words.

chapter one

The Messenger

IN THE BOOK *ALCOHOLICS ANONYMOUS*, Bill W. introduces us to Ebby T as part of his own first-person account, "Bill's Story." He puts it this way:

> *My musing was interrupted by the telephone. The cheery voice of an old school friend asked if he might come over. He was sober.*

This schoolmate was, of course, Ebby T.

When Ebby contacted Bill on that November night in 1934, Bill was drunk — Ebby was sober. Ebby wanted to carry his personal message of how he had found sobriety, and perhaps the Oxford Group message as well, to Bill.

Bill elaborates in his Big Book story:

> *The door opened and he stood there, fresh-skinned and glowing. There was something about his eyes. He was inexplicably different. What had happened?*

Bill goes on to tell how his friend refused his offer of a drink, which disappointed him.

"Come, what's all this about?" I queried.

He looked straight at me. Simply, but smilingly, he said, "I've got religion." [4]

In telling his story, Bill describes his personal prejudices toward religion. But Ebby said something that seemed to turn Bill around.

My friend suggested what then seemed to be a novel idea. He said, "Why don't you choose your own conception of God?"

That statement hit me hard. It melted the icy intellectual mountain in whose shadow I had lived and shivered many years. I stood in the sunlight at last. [5]

Ebby didn't achieve permanent sobriety immediately. He was what was referred to as a "slipper" or an "in and outer." Throughout his life he had periods of time with continuous, seemingly happy sobriety. Most of these occurred while he was living in Texas during the 1950s.

The following account is based completely on Ebby's own words, extracted from eight separate recordings and combined here. [6]

It was November 1934 and I was living back in New York with my friend Shep Cornell in his 57th Street apartment, which was a welcome relief to me. Through the help of the Oxford Group I had been sober for about six weeks. It was the first time I'd been in New York sober in over ten years.

I knew some of the guys who were working on Wall Street. One day I decided to pay them a visit. During my visit I learned through a friend of Bill Wilson's sister-in-law that Bill was in rough shape because of his drinking. The man suggested that I might call on Bill to see if there was anything I could do to help. Of course I was eager to see my old friend, but I knew I had better be very cautious. I felt Bill would either want to dive into this Oxford Group thing lock, stock, and barrel or he would have nothing to do with it. No middle of the road for Wilson — he'd either take it all or nothing. I prayed and thought deeply about how to approach Bill, fearful of turning him off. Trying to decide exactly how I would explain it all to Bill was a painstaking procedure.

Finally I called over to the Wilson house and Lois answered the phone. I explained what had happened to me and that I was staying sober through the Oxford Group. Of course I mentioned to her I had been sober a little less than two months. Lois invited me to dinner and we scheduled a date.

At 5:30 on the appointed afternoon I arrived at the Wilson house at 182 Clinton Street in Brooklyn. I was greeted by "Green," who I remembered as a servant of Lois's family for many years. Nobody else was home at the time, but Bill arrived shortly thereafter. He had been drinking, but wasn't too bad. We sat a bit, and then Bill had to scoot out for some ice cream. A short time later he left to get something for their dinner. I knew and understood why Bill was taking these short trips by himself — he needed a drink.

Some time had passed and Lois arrived home along with the girl who lived upstairs who had also been invited to dinner. After dinner we moved upstairs to the living room for a visit. Lois finally interrupted the small talk and asked me to tell them all about what had been going on with me.

This was my opportunity, exactly what I had been waiting for! With as much excitement and enthusiasm as I think I've ever had, I began to tell them my story. I talked about my problems with drinking and the law, and how the men from the Oxford Group had come to see me. I shared much of what I had been learning from the Oxford Group — that by turning my problems over to God as I understood God, I found release from my obsession to drink. I was so wound up that night that I talked until one o'clock in the morning.

At the conclusion of the evening, Bill volunteered to walk me to the subway. This time it wasn't an attempt by him to get a drink because he had a bottle in the house. I guess it must have impressed him because he walked to the subway . . .

suddenly he put his arm around my shoulder and said, "I don't know what you've got but I want it."

. . . I was born in 1896 in Albany, New York, to a large, affluent, and prominent family. We spent our summers in Manchester, Vermont, where my family rented a cottage. It was a short sixty-mile train ride from our Albany home, but I always like to tell the story of my first automobile ride from Albany to Manchester. My older brothers and father had built the car in my father's foundry machine shop. The trip took three days and the car broke down several times before finally completely giving out on top of a hill about four miles south of town. We had to have the car hauled in by a team of horses. I can still see the town constable yelling to us, "Get a horse! Get a horse!"

It was in Manchester that I met Bill Wilson and Lois Burnham. The Burnhams had a place directly across from where my family rented our cottage. Lois was a few years older than I was and she could remember when I was still in a baby carriage.

One summer it was decided that I would stay behind in Manchester to attend "Burr and Burton Academy." I had been attending the "Albany Academy," a private military school in Albany. Even though Bill and I had previously met, it was at Burr and Burton that we really became friends during the 1912 school year.

After just one year at Burr and Burton, I returned to Albany Academy. I was set back a year because the school wouldn't recognize my year at Burr and Burton. It was around that time that I first started drinking, although for the most part it was controlled drinking.

I do recall one event in which drinking almost got me into trouble. After a competitive drill, a bunch of us decided to go out and get drunk. We got into a mess and the school principal heard about it. Fortunately for me, nothing was said and there were no immediate repercussions.

My parents took me out of school early that spring because I had been quite ill. By the beginning of the summer, my father received a letter from the school principal who had always called me "Ed." The letter informed my father that there was nothing more the school could do with "Ed." It was a nice way of saying that I had been expelled from school.

My father was in the iron-foundry business, so when fall approached he told me, "You're going to work at the foundry." I was hired as a molder's helper, which was fairly rugged work.

I worked very hard every day, getting up at 6:00 a.m. to be there early. On Saturday nights I liked to drink and at that time most of my drinking was confined to Saturdays. However, when the holidays came around with all of the festivities I couldn't contain myself. Saturday night drinking turned into drinking at parties, dances, and every other opportunity. The drinking really seemed to help me socialize, especially with the girls.

I remember being concerned about drinking very early on. Once I had a conversation with Bill Wilson about drinking while we were together at school. That was before either of us had yet taken the first drink. Even then, I thought highly enough of Bill to confide some of my personal fears growing up surrounded by problem drinkers. Bill and I bonded, perhaps because of alcoholism since the condition was in both of our families. My brothers and father all drank too much and I thought I might be like them, at least in temperament. Of course, I feared that I might go the same way.

I remember my first drink in a public place was in a bar at a local hotel, and I ordered a glass of beer. It was the finest beer I had ever had and the warm glow I felt afterwards made me decide, "This is for me." I had always been uncomfortable around people and especially in crowds. I found that having a few drinks would loosen me up and make me feel like "the kingpin," which is apparently what I always wanted to be. Feelings of inadequacy and fear stuck with me throughout my life and drinking seemed to bring about at least a temporary relief.

The problem I faced was that I could never predict how much I would drink or what would happen. Sometimes I could drink the other guys under the table. Other times after only a few drinks, I was swinging from chandeliers.

My drinking became progressively worse. Over the next twenty years I found myself getting in various scrapes, losing jobs, and feeling remorseful. Eventually I read a book by Richard Peabody entitled *The Common Sense of Drinking.* One particular section really stuck with me. It was an explanation of the difference between a "hard drinker" and an "alcoholic." Even though both people might drink the same amount on any given night, the "hard drinker" would awaken the next morning to *just another day* and immediately focus on his responsibilities for the day ahead. The "alcoholic" awoke to thoughts of the night before and how he could get the next drink to bring the party back.

That was the way it always was for me — forget business, I wanted to get with the gang and party again. *The Common Sense of Drinking* also explained that alcohol affects certain people differently than others. For them, alcohol is too fascinating and they can't handle it. I could see I fit into this group. This information, coupled with the effect alcohol had on my family, convinced me that I should not drink. But that intellectual knowledge wasn't enough to get me to stop once I had started. But I believed it to be true, as did Bill W. who later used information in the Peabody book in his writing of the Big Book.

In 1922, the family business broke up after seventy years in existence. Consequently, I found myself out of a job. I located another one, but bounced from one job to the next as my drinking continued to worsen. Eventually I found myself enlisted in a unit of the National Guard. I was stationed locally working at the armory in Albany as a second lieutenant during World War I. I enjoyed this period of time because drink was readily available to me. During Prohibition time one needed a prescription to buy a pint of whiskey. There was a druggist nearby who kept the officers' quarters supplied with gallons of whiskey.

Most of the guys I worked with at that time were older than I was. It seemed all of them liked drinking and they were some of the best two-fisted drinkers I have ever known. One night I, along with some of my drinking pals, got plastered drunk and somehow got into a serious accident with a taxi. I was banged up and bloodied pretty badly. My father found me the next morning sitting on the edge of my bed, still bleeding, and gave me an ultimatum: either go down to the National Guard and resign or get out of the house. That afternoon I turned in my resignation, thus ending my short-lived military career.

Bill Wilson and I remained friends through the years; however, we saw each other only occasionally during the summers. In the late 1920s I was briefly involved in the investment business. I worked in an Albany office for a New York firm at the same time Bill W. worked on Wall Street. Bill came to Albany on a business trip and looked me up.

We met downtown for some drinks. *It was the first and only time Bill and I ever got drunk together.* I took Bill all over town that night, drinking everywhere we went. We finally ended up at a party with a bunch of my friends: "fliers" as I liked to call them. They were actually known as "barnstormers" and were the daredevils of their day. Bill needed to get back to Vermont and I thought it was a grand idea to get one of my friends to fly us up to Manchester. Consequently, we chartered a plane and my pal Ted Burke agreed to pilot. It was the very first flight to ever land at the Manchester air field. When the town's people heard about it, everyone — including the town band — came out to meet the plane. Once it landed both Bill and I staggered off, falling on the ground drunk, embarrassing ourselves in front of all the onlookers.

Things continued to get worse for me. My mother passed away in 1927, and my father died in 1929. I inherited money after my father's death, but what I didn't squander away drinking I lost in the stock market crash.

By the spring of 1934, I moved into my family's vacant house in Manchester. After renting a cottage for many years, my parents had finally bought the place in 1923. Most of the furniture had been divided up among my married brothers and I was left with one furnished room. I lived there alone, and appeared to be drinking myself to a certain death in the not-too-distant future.

Within just a few months, I got in trouble with the law twice. The first time it was for driving my car into the kitchen of a woman's house while drunk. The lady was quite shaken up over the ordeal. I stepped out of the car and politely asked her if I could trouble her for a cup of coffee.

Another time after drinking heavily, I decided I wanted to rid the house of pigeons. It was dark out and, believe me, it was pouring down rain, so I loaded the old double-barreled shotgun and I went out and I was backing up . . . to get a shot at them. [The lawn was wet from all the rain.] Down I went and landed on my back. There I was lying on my back and I didn't see any reason to get up and shoot at them, so I was banging away from the ground. I guess my neighbors could see me and I imagine they complained to the law.

In late July or early August, two old drinking friends of mine came by my house to pay me a visit. Their names were Cebra Graves and Shepard (Shep) Cornell. Both of them were heavy drinkers, although I didn't consider them to be alcoholic — at least not like I was. They made small talk for a while until finally the guys began to tell me about an organization they had joined called the Oxford Group. They said they had found a great deal of help by using the spiritual values of the group and they had straightened out their lives.

Cebra and Shep suggested that I consider turning my life over to *"God as I understood Him."* The more they talked, the more impressed I became. Most of the information those two shared wasn't altogether new. I was familiar with most of the information because of my religious upbringing. I agreed to give it a try and my friends left me with a book to read, an inspiring story of how a businessman successfully overcame his drinking problem. I totally identified with the story and I could really see myself in the pages of the book.

Author's note: *Ebby was unable to recall the book's title, but his description suggests it was* I Was a Pagan, *a 1934 book by Victor Kitchen.*

The Oxford Group was not an organization that concentrated on helping alcoholics; it was a spiritual group founded by a minister from Pennsylvania named Frank Buchman. The group got its name because Buchman took a "team" of young men mostly from Oxford University to do mission work in South Africa. While they were there, the press became quite curious about them. In an article one of the reporters referred to them as the "Oxford Group" and the name stuck. The group's focus wasn't on helping drunks. Their interest was in "changing lives"; and if it [the life] happened to be [that of] a drunk — so be it.

Around this time I realized the house needed painting. The problem was I couldn't get to the top of the house, though, because my ladder wasn't tall enough. I contacted my brother who gave me permission to hire a local painter to come and help with the house. I stayed sober for a couple of weeks while we finished up the painting job. It seemed easy for me to stop drinking while I was busy working on the house. But as soon as it was completed and I was left with nothing to do, I went right back to the bottle.

In Vermont at that time there was a law that anyone arrested three times within one year would serve a mandatory six months in jail. I had been drunk in public, along with the two earlier incidents, so I had three strikes against me and the law was looking for me. I spent a lot of time locked in the house to drink so I couldn't be arrested until I decided to go into town. Once I did, the local constable apprehended me and took me to Bennington to see the judge. It was a Friday afternoon and the judge happened to be the father of Cebra, one of the two men who had called on me a few weeks earlier. He told me to be back in court on Monday and to be sober. The constable dropped me off at home and reminded me what the judge had said about being sober on Monday.

Once home, I remembered I had three cold bottles of Ballantine Ale in the basement. I started thinking about how I could nurse those three bottles over the weekend and still appear in court on Monday sober. I went downstairs for a bottle but began to think what I was doing wasn't being honest. What the judge had really meant was "Don't drink."

So I headed back up the stairs resolved to not touch the beer. It was as if a little tiny devil stood on my shoulder telling me, "It's okay, go ahead and drink." A while later, after three or four trips up and down the stairs, l was driving myself crazy and finally surrendered. l grabbed a sack, put the three bottles in it, and gave them to a neighbor.

And believe me that was a weight that was lifted off my shoulder . . . l felt a release from that time on. . . . And l know that night l sat down beside my bed and said my prayers like l hadn't said them in years. l said to God . . . , "l really mean this, l want to quit this drinking." l hadn't prayed like this ever before; l hadn't prayed much at all for a very long time.

The following Monday when l appeared in court l was met by my two friends from the Oxford Group. This time they had another guy with them, Rowland Hazard. l had never met him before. Judge Graves agreed to release me on my own recognizance with the understanding l would be in Rowland's custody. Rowland, who was also alcoholic, had spent some time abroad in Switzerland where he had been under the treatment of the famed psychiatrist Dr. Carl Jung. The treatment failed and Rowland found himself drunk again. He was later able to quit drinking through the Oxford Group.

Rowland invited me to stay with him for a few weeks. We took roads trips throughout Vermont, speaking various places about the Oxford Group. The first weekend l spoke five times: at two churches, a junior college, and two town meetings. This went on for a few weeks and sometimes a few of the guys from New York would join us and we would attend "house parties" put on by the Oxford Group.

After a few weeks, Rowland took me to New York where l stayed with Shep while he made arrangements for me to move into Calvary Mission operated by the Calvary Episcopal Church. At the time it was the headquarters for the Oxford Group in America. l soon became one of what was called "a brotherhood of twelve men" and we ran the mission. There were enough beds for thirty-five men and they were filled every night.

l believe that the popularity of the Oxford Group stemmed from the stock market crash in 1929. People had lost everything and were searching for something. Many had been worshipping or paying devotion to false gods and just weren't on track. A great many alcoholics, or drunkards as they were called then, were included among the growing number of Oxford Groupers.

I threw myself into the group whole heartedly and wanted to learn everything. They had some excellent and very wise teachers who indoctrinated me very well. The leader of the group in America was the Reverend Samuel M. Shoemaker Jr. He was the rector of the Calvary Episcopal Church.

I continued to stay sober by using the precepts I was learning through the group and by attempting to be of service to others. I've always felt that some of these non-alcoholic Oxford Groupers were very effective and successful working with the alcoholics.

This brings me up to November 1934 when I called over to the Wilson house and ultimately had my meeting with Bill. His memory of the events from that evening is rather different than mine. I think the main points are the same, but his view of some of the specifics is a bit garbled. Nevertheless, walking to the subway, he said, "I don't know what you've got kid — but you've got something and I want to get it."

Like me, Bill didn't stop drinking immediately, but the seed had been planted. About two nights later Bill showed up at the Calvary Mission just before meeting time. He arrived with a merchant marine, and they were both visibly drunk. It was a testimonial type meeting where the leader called on different people to come up front and share. On that particular evening Bill had something he wanted to get off his chest. He stood up, walked to the front, rested his elbow on the piano, and began making a speech. The superintendent tried to get me to stop Bill from going up, but I insisted, "Let him go — let's see what he's got to say." Bill didn't really have anything of great significance to share that night, but it was apparent that I had made a strong impression on him.

A few days later Bill showed up at Towns Hospital, and, waving a bottle of beer he told his doctor that this time he had something. Dr. Silkworth replied, "You sure do, Bill. Now go on up and sleep it off."

I called on Bill several times while he was in the hospital and answered Bill's questions about the Oxford Group as best I could. It was during that hospital [stay] that Bill W. had his "spiritual experience" and was freed from alcohol, never to return to the bottle again.

I "rode herd" on Bill in the beginning and stuck by him as we attended many Oxford Group meetings. Bill quickly got comfortable and started speaking at meetings as time went on. Those early meetings we attended were basically the same as the AA meetings of today. Everyone had the opportunity to share their experience, strength, and hope. Of course, the meetings weren't confined to alcoholics, but those attending shared their problems and their victories.

Bill traveled to Akron on a business venture in May of 1935. The trip resulted in him meeting Dr. Bob Smith and the founding of Alcoholics Anonymous. Bill stayed several extra months in Akron working with Dr. Bob to try to sober up some of the patients from Akron City Hospital. I continued my work in New York through the Oxford Group.

I was really trying to live by the teachings I had learned in the Oxford Group. The Oxford Group was based on a return to first-century Christian fellowship. We had four so-called principles somewhat similar to the Twelve Steps of Alcoholics Anonymous. These were absolute honesty, absolute love, absolute unselfishness, and absolute purity. Now, of course, these are broken down into workable, everyday living.

The Oxford Group advocated the principle of morning meditation, or as they called it "quiet time," when one tried to release the self to get in tune with "God as you understood Him" — to try to get some guidance for the day ahead and to hold yourself flexible — not make any set plans whenever it was possible to do so. Then one should try to meet each situation as it came up and meet it believing that it was God's will that the events shall transpire as they do — in other words, to accept what comes each day.

A few months after Bill returned to New York, he invited me to come live with him and Lois on Clinton Street. I stayed with them for a year. While I was living with Bill, we had meetings for the alcoholics at the house. The meetings "stuck" for some of them and we began having successful recoveries. Unfortunately, I remember one chap committed suicide and we all took that hard. After a while we started a meeting at Steinway Hall in New York.

By the summer of 1936, after nearly two years of sober life in New York City, I decided to move back to Albany where I had made such a mess of my life. I felt the need to begin making amends and paying restitution to the people I had harmed. I also needed to start earning some money.

Shortly after returning to Albany, I was hired by Ford Motor Company in Green Island, about eight miles north of Albany. I worked for two weeks on the day shift and then two weeks on the night shift. That gave me a long weekend after the night-shift schedule. That's when I would head back to New York to see friends and attend meetings. This went on for a while, but I started slowly pulling away from doing the things that were keeping me on track. I began to feel lonely and sorry for myself, blaming God for not giving me the one thing I really wanted — a romantic relationship with someone I could love. Somehow I felt I'd been mistreated.

One day a friend from work commented that I hadn't been myself and described me as "a piece of steel wire." I headed to New York that weekend and checked into the Lexington Hotel. It was April of 1937 and I had been sober for more than two and a half years — a record for me.

There was a girl in New York that I enjoyed visiting, and we went to dinner that weekend as we often did when I was in town. We weren't romantically involved, just close friends. At dinner that night she ordered a scotch highball as she normally did. It had never bothered me before, but this time I ordered one for myself, much to the surprise of my friend. She questioned what I was doing and, of course, I rationalized the drink. By midnight she was so disgusted with me she had a taxi drop me off at my hotel. I was roaring drunk.

Back at the hotel I called Bill and the next morning he sent a couple of guys over to pick me up and take me to Bill's house.

Bill was gone for the weekend but told me there was a bottle of scotch in the house in case I needed to overcome the jitters while coming off the drunk. I figured since I had started drinking I might as well finish the job. I spent the rest of the weekend drunk at Wilson's home.

On Monday I showed up late at work. The superintendent met me at the time clock and asked me where I had been. I explained to him I had been in New York for the weekend and ended up with a bad case of ptomaine poisoning. My boss told me to get in there and get busy.

I headed to my work area where the supervisor told me a crane had broken and they needed me to help unload a car load of flat steel by hand. By the end of the day, I was sick from a hangover and could barely open my hands after hauling the heavy flat steel.

At that time I was riding to and from work with another guy so we could split expenses. When we left that day, my friend told me he had tried to raise a few dollars so he could take me out for a few badly needed drinks. He apologized because he had been unable to come up with any money. I said, "Never mind getting the money. I've got some money. Now let's just go to a tavern."

That ended my job at Ford Motor Company. A few days later a security man showed up with a paycheck for one day of work and asked for my employee badge. For the next fifteen years I bounced in and out of AA and various alcoholic guest homes finding only brief periods of sobriety.

I spent a summer at Joy Farm, which later became High Watch Farm in Kent, Connecticut. It was founded in 1940 and was the first alcoholic rehabilitation health farm in the country. I stayed there several more times during the 1940s and even worked there on several occasions, eventually becoming the assistant manager. I did well during my time there; again — when I was busy and had a purpose — things seemed to go along just fine. When the manager left for a job at Beech Hill in Dublin, New Hampshire, I followed and worked with him there for about a year in 1949.

From there it was back to New York. I stayed at Chester Cook Home for Intemperate Men, which was similar to the work farms of the day. I would work on the farm during the day and go to meetings every night and twice on Sundays. I knew what I needed to be doing and when I was taking the right action things worked out. But my thinking would get screwed up and I would find myself drunk again. I knew the answers but just couldn't apply them. This was powerlessness for me and my condition continued to worsen.

After spending the summer of 1953 floundering around New York, drunk most of the time, I decided to drop by the AA Intergroup Office in hopes of putting "the touch" on somebody for enough money to get a bottle and a flop. I wanted to get back in AA. I was trying to get back, but I just didn't have any reason to live — nothing to keep me going.

At the Intergroup Office one of the women, Hazel R., saw me and said, "There's a guy who's been wanting to talk to you; his name is Charlie M. He's got something for you." Then Hazel called Charlie — he told her to keep me from leaving until he could get there around five o'clock.

Late that afternoon Charlie picked me up and took me out for a drink. While I sat there drinking, Charlie told me that he traveled extensively for work and during the summer he had been in Paris. While attending a small AA meeting, one of the guys found out that Charlie was from New York. He asked Charlie how I was doing. The guy happened to be Cebra G., who had helped me all those years ago. Charlie told Cebra he didn't personally know me, but he had heard I wasn't doing very well. Cebra said that he knew I was having a great deal of trouble and was "under a blanket of despair." He asked that Charlie somehow find me and get me out of New York. Charlie gave Cebra his word and those were not mere words. I've always been very grateful to Charlie.

After explaining all this, Charlie told me that he used to live in Dallas and there were some guys there who might be able to help me. He asked me if I would consider going to Texas. My immediate response was not favorable, but Charlie persisted. He gave me enough money for some food, a flop, and a bottle. Charlie told me he'd be back the next night to discuss it further.

I got a room at the Mills Hotel, which was admittedly a pretty grim place to sleep. I also got myself a bottle but wasn't much interested in food. When Charlie returned the following evening, a Thursday, he again bought me some drinks and suggested I consider taking him up on the Texas offer. He also gave me his address and enough money for the night and said, "If you decide you want to go, come and see me."

Well, I nursed the money along and didn't see Charlie on Friday but thought about his offer. I knew or at least I believed that I was going to die alone there in New York and rationalized to myself I might as well die in Texas, rather than on the streets of New York. On Saturday morning I made my way to Charlie's apartment where I was able to get cleaned up and was given some fresh clothes to wear. . . . I asked him if there was anything he wanted to do so that night he called up Oley L. and Oley said, "Send the Yankee son-of-a-bitch down." I knew those were the exact words because I could hear Oley's booming voice through the phone.

On Sunday evening, September 6, 1953, Charlie loaded me sober onto an American Airlines nonstop flight to Dallas Love Field. I later found out he had a pint in his pocket, but because I was already sober he decided not to give it to me. Boy, I sure could have used the pint! When I arrived in Texas, I was taken to the Texas Clinic in very bad condition. I spent the next several weeks coming off my nearly three-month drunk, experiencing hallucinations, delirium tremens, and intervals of unconsciousness. Searcy W., the director, said that it was uncertain at times whether or not I would live and, if I did pull through, just how much brain damage I might have suffered.

One night I got out of the clinic and was taking a walk while still experiencing hallucinations. I was picked up by the police and had a terrible time explaining myself. They finally called Icky S. who came down, explained things to the officers, and took me back to the clinic. I was very glad to see Icky that night.

When I finally started becoming coherent, I didn't believe I
was in Texas. One of the ladies working at the clinic had to run
some errands one afternoon and decided to take me along for the
ride. We stopped by the airport to mail a letter and I saw the sign
for Love Field. I was able to touch the sign and finally believed I
was actually in Texas.

During my several-month stay at the Texas Clinic, I really felt
like a dignitary; so many AA people came to meet me and talk
with me. Certainly my celebrity status was due to the fact that I
was the one who carried *the message* to Bill Wilson. I loved the
attention and really enjoyed my time in Texas. I was able to get
out and take short trips with some of the AA guys. AA in Texas
was really growing at that time and groups were springing up all
over. A new group would start and members from some of the
more established groups would drive to the new group and offer
support. I was able to go on many of those trips and on a few occasions would share my experiences related to the early days.

The Texas State Convention was held in June of 1954 and Bill
Wilson came to speak. He thanked the people of Texas for all they
had been doing for me — his "sponsor." I also spoke for a few minutes at the convention and enjoyed my time with my friend Bill
W. My relationship with Bill was very good. Bill always publicly
referred to me as his sponsor.

Author's note: *Many of the Texas AA people said that Bill W.'s love
and deep gratitude toward Ebby were obvious, as were Ebby's toward Bill.
Bill's gratitude to Charlie for making it possible for Ebby to be in Texas
was also obvious.*

After thirteen months of sobriety in Texas, I did have a slip. As best
I can remember, I just got off the beam and away I went. It didn't
get too bad, though, thanks to Bill Decker, the sheriff, by means of
the county jail. I went from the city jail to the county, then back
to the city. It wasn't much of a mission at all. I'd get out and they
would pick me up again and back in I would go. Believe me, you
can't look crosswise at a drink in Dallas or you're getting in jail.

I've always counted my sobriety by counting the time l wasn't drinking. l don't believe that because l had slips l have lost the sobriety l have already experienced. Of course, this may just be my own rationalization, but it's my opinion. My sobriety record clearly had interruptions; my longest consecutive period of sobriety was immediately after my *slip* in Texas. l was able to put together close to seven years. During those years in Texas l held several jobs, became quite active in my attendance at AA meetings, and spoke quite a bit throughout Texas and neighboring states. l was a guest speaker at two of AA's international conventions, though l have never considered myself to be much of an orator.

At one of the conferences, an attendee approached me and said, "So much is said, done, and written for the new man, but very little for the person who has trouble off and on. Especially for the old grey-beards or bleeding deacons or whatever you want to call them."

l responded in my talk the next day by saying the following: "Certainly l can qualify to talk on that thing, but l don't know if l can give you any information that is valuable. l sometimes think the reason we stay drunk so long — people who have had a long record of sobriety and then fall off — is, first, our pride is hurt. l think that is one of the biggest things. We're not so sorry that we hurt somebody . . . But we are sorry that that wonderful record we have is gone. And l think it just galls us to believe that we can't up and be the little bit of a big operator we've been. That's just one theory. And second, of course, is the fact that when you start on one of those things, that little old devil that's still in me and always will be l guess until l die says, 'Now that you've started the thing you might just as well make a good one out of it.' And that's exactly what you do — you keep it up."

In that particular talk l also attempted to share points about my own drinking. "l don't have trouble daily or every few days the way that some people say they do about taking a drink, or wanting to take a drink. It does come back once in a while, sometimes in the springtime or in the fall; l don't know if it's the change of seasons or what it is — you got to blame it on something. You know what Omar Khayyám said: 'Come, fill the Cup, and in the fire of spring, the winter garment of repentance fling.'"

I always used to believe in that. Come spring if I had been on the wagon for a few months I always had to have my spring drunk. So that's all there was to that. But I don't know what makes us fall off the wagon again — drink again after we have been sober for a number of years. It is undoubtedly due to wrong thinking and that wrong thinking can sneak in sometimes and get so set in your mind that you don't recognize it. I know that I've had a number of drunks as I look back on it now where I was drunk mentally a long time before I took a drink.

In time I was able to get to the point where I could recognize this type of thinking and do something about it before I picked up the drink. I was able to "think the drink through" before taking it and know what was going to happen if I didn't change my thinking. It was like walking through a bunch of doors and each door that you go through things continue to get worse all the time, each door taking you closer to drinking.

During most of the time I was in Texas, I lived with Ralph and Mary Lou Jones in Ozona after leaving the clinic in 1953. I enjoyed fishing and had developed some friendships with the AA people. I worked several jobs while in Texas and bought a car and paid for it on time, which I was quite proud of. I even found a girlfriend. Her name was Chloe and I met her at the Texas Clinic where she worked.

Author's note: Mel B. shares information about Ebby and Chloe's relationship in his book Ebby: The Man Who Sponsored Bill W. *His research suggests that Ebby fell in love, perhaps blindly, but Chloe was not deeply in love with Ebby. Although details are sketchy, it is commonly known that Ebby returned to the bottle the day after Chloe's death.*

Bill deeply loved Ebby for having carried the message to him. He extended every bit of kindness and gratitude toward him that he could. On no less than two occasions for periods of more than a year, Ebby moved in with Bill and Lois. Later on, when Ebby's health was failing, Bill asked for assistance in providing money to help care for Ebby.

Bill wrote the following letter to some of his AA friends.

December 1, 1961

Dear Friend in A.A.,

This concerns the future welfare of our great friend — and my sponsor — Edwin T. He's better known to thousands of us as Ebby. He is the one who, in November 1934, brought the message to me that later became the essence of A.A.'s Twelve Steps, a message that has saved the lives of countless others since. Ebby therefore occupies a unique position in our affection and gratitude.

For many years Ebby had his ups and downs with alcohol. But about seven years ago, immensely helped by Texas A.A. friends, he made his full recovery and has since stayed sober under trying conditions in his own life. He has made a wonderful demonstration; something that has inspired all who have witnessed it. For myself, I count Ebby's final recovery as one of the happiest events of my entire A.A. career.

Such is the background for what I now wish to outline:

The fact is that Ebby needs some financial assistance. Because of his declining health due to a progressive lung ailment, he is presently going to need more than the relatively small amount of money which he has been receiving from a few friends.

Though he is still employed, his earnings are so meager that recently the Trustees of the General Service Board allotted him $100 a month to supplement his income. This sum is being paid out of the earnings of our A.A. books. Should he become too ill to work — and this could occur at any time — I feel that the Trustees would then be disposed to grant him enough extra to carry his living expenses under such a condition.

But this income would not prove to be enough to carry the medical expenses of a serious and lengthy illness — something that may well develop.

Accordingly, I am sponsoring an effort to raise $5,000 to take care of such an emergency. It would clearly be undesirable to solicit A.A. as a whole for such a sum. Even though Ebby's case is completely unique, we nevertheless might, by such a solicitation, create an unwanted precedent.

Therefore this special fund for him is a matter for two or three dozen of us to handle on a strictly "one shot" anonymous basis — each of us contributing, let us say, $200 apiece. Your name has been suggested to me as one who might be very happy to make such a gift.

We have already set up a special account on our General Service Board books designated as: "T Fund" (last name omitted with respect to AA's tradition of anonymity). However, please draw your check to the "General Fund" or "General Service Board of A.A.," and mail it care of: General Service Board of A.A., 305 E. 45th Street, New York 17, N.Y. I shall acknowledge each contribution, and render you yearly statements. It is also agreed that any finally unused portion of this Fund will be given to A.A. World Services, Inc. as a "group" contribution to A.A.'s global service effort. Your gift will of course be tax deductible.

You will be glad to know that a few of these special contributions are already on deposit, and it is my earnest hope that your own will presently increase the total.

Most gratefully yours,

Bill[7]

It seems appropriate to conclude Ebby's story by sharing the recollections of others. Ebby didn't stay much longer in Texas. Money from Bill W.'s special fund was used to get Ebby back up to New York. Ebby's health had been failing — he developed a lung condition (emphysema) due to years of heavy smoking. Again, he floundered for several years staying with family members and with the Wilsons. He was finally moved to McPike Farm in upstate New York, where he lived out the remainder of his life. Margaret McPike wrote the following letter, dated March 26, 1966, five days after Ebby's death.

My Dear Dorthea,

It is with deepest regret that I am returning your letter to you. Our dear friend passed away on Monday, last, March 21. As you may have heard he made his home here with us since May 30, 1964 when Bill brought him from High Watch Farm, at that time a very sick man. However, he gradually improved to the point where he was up for lunch most every day, rest, and down for dinner, sometimes staying down until 9 or 9:30, which he did the night before he was taken sick. He was not feeling himself early in the A.M. and after Doctor came said he probably should go into the hospital in the P.M. if he wasn't feeling better, for tests. However, he started going into cardiac failure and we are fortunate to have a little hospital nearby, within five miles, and ambulance service. I spent most of the next four days with him. He became semi-comatose most of the time but did know me Saturday and Saturday evening. After that he did not respond to anyone.

For many things I am thankful, mostly that he did not suffer long and when we had to leave him Thursday, he like so many surely looked and made all of us feel, that he was surely at peace.

My home seems very empty; he was part of my family and as you probably know did not talk frequently, but when he did it was meaningful and with an original sense of humor. My husband and I met and have been married since we came into AA some (13) years. For the past seven years we have maintained our home as a rest home for many and were glad we had been able to maintain the sobriety that was given to us, that in some way we could help

Ebbie [sic]*, knowing well if it had not been for him, this might not have been possible for us.*

Ebbie often spoke of his friends in Texas and I know he had wonderful memories of the friendship there and the good years he had with you people. It is a small world and who knows one day we will meet, either you coming in my direction or I might be in yours. I made it to Nevada two years ago, but never to Texas yet. However, I am a nurse, hoping or wishfully thinking of a few days in Kentucky this year and when Convention time comes someday we may have one in Houston. I shall be happy to hear from you whenever possible. I know we will be sharing thoughts of Ebbie frequently.

Most Sincerely,

Margaret McPike [8]

Many rumors have been heard over the years about Ebby. First is the myth that Ebby's ongoing difficulty with the bottle was somehow due to an unshakable resentment toward Bill Wilson and Dr. Bob Smith for not considering him as a founder or cofounder of Alcoholics Anonymous. Second is the rumor that he died drunk. Third is the issue of his sobriety, and whether or not he really made any significant contributions to the founding of AA.

After a great deal of research, I have come to believe that Ebby held no resentment toward Bill W. or Dr. Bob. He always seemed to have tremendous gratitude to God for having been selected to carry a message of hope to Bill W. The above letter offers proof that while staying at the McPike Farm Ebby was sober for over two years and died sober.

Regarding Ebby's contribution to the founding of the AA program, it is likely that he was more influential on Bill W. than anyone will ever really know. Ebby was extremely well read, a fact that is often overlooked. He and Bill W. spent a great deal of time together from December 1934 through April 1937. We know from Bill's story that Ebby introduced him to the Oxford

Group steps. Ebby also shared several books with Bill, including William James's *Varieties of Religious Experience* and Richard Peabody's *The Common Sense of Drinking*.

It's likely that Bill and his sponsor Ebby spent many nights in the Wilson home on Clinton Street sharing coffee and discussing the ideas that somehow made their way into the book *Alcoholics Anonymous*.

chapter two

"If There Is a God, Will He Show Himself?"

YOU'VE READ EBBY'S VERSION OF HIS LIFE STORY and his description of what took place in the Wilson home in November 1934. Now I'd like to share Bill W.'s version of events prior to his business trip to Akron. Throughout his life Bill must have told the story of AA's early days and his own personal story hundreds of times. His description of his spiritual experience and the events leading up to it was very consistent, although at times he focused on different aspects of the story, probably to suit his audience. This chapter includes several versions of Bill's spiritual experience, as related by Bill. The first was presented to a group in Chicago in 1951.

> Everyone in this audience has had his great hour of realization. Every alcoholic here has come to the identical path that I did, the realization that I was utterly unable to go on living; that I was in the grip of an obsession which my own resources could not break. How well I remember my first realization of that stark dilemma. It was in the summer of 1934. I lay in Towns Hospital in New York. The good doctor there at my other visits had been encouraging but now he sat speaking to Lois downstairs. And she was inquiring, "Why, oh why, can't he get well, Doctor? His willpower is strong enough in other things. Why can't he break this insanity?"

And the doctor proceeded to explain to her that my obsession was indeed the master of my will. And it condemned me to go on drinking against anything that I could do or that medical science could do that he knew of. So Lois, like every wife here, had her hour of realization that I was hopeless.

3   Then came an interval of a few months. And during that period a friend of mine who had been released of his obsession by the grace of God came to visit me. And over my kitchen table where I sat drinking while Lois was at work, he related the simple formula which has now flowered into our Twelve Steps of recovery. And that simple essence was, you remember, that he admitted that he couldn't manage his own life. That he had got honest with himself as never before. That he had made a confession of his character defects. That he had tried to sweep away the debris of the past and was mending his broken relations with others. And then he told me of a new kind of giving that demanded no rewards. And then, rather hesitantly, because he knew my agnosticism, he said that to do these things "I asked God's help." Thus spoke one alcoholic to another in a kitchen basement on Clinton Street in Brooklyn in November 1934.

I rebelled against his idea of God. But somehow, the memory of that conversation could never escape me. He didn't stay long; presently he was through—leaving me to my thoughts. And in no waking hour after, could I banish what he said from my mind. There was no new principle that he had annunciated; of course there wasn't. But why did these simple precepts stick when poured into me by him?

Well, you and I know as I didn't realize then. We know that he impressed me because he presented a spectacle of release. We knew that I was impressed; we know now that I was impressed because he was another alcoholic. He spoke my language. And so a realization came that maybe there was hope.

At length I returned again to the hospital to be cleared up. The doctor put me to bed. I wasn't yet in such a bad way. Three days later, free from sedative and alcohol, I looked up one morning out of my depression and saw this friend standing in the door. I feared he would evangelize me, but no, he didn't.

He said he heard I was there — just came to pay a friendly visit. I asked him once more what the terms of his release were. Quite simply he stated them, and again he took himself away. Well, when he had gone my depression deepened, until it seemed that I was in the bottom of a pit.

For you see I still rebelled against the idea that there would be a God who could save me; who could enable me to do what I couldn't do myself. But presently my rebellion ceased and in an agony I cried out, "If there is a God, will He show Himself?"

And then came an experience which, of course, is the great event of my whole life. I had a very sudden experience in which it seemed that the room lighted up. I was caught into a great ecstasy. It seemed as though I were on top of the mountain and a great wind blew. And I knew it was Spirit. And at length I found myself still on the bed, now surrounded by a Presence. And I thought to myself, "So this is the God of the preachers."

You yourselves have had exactly the same kind of things happen to you, excepting that it took longer. But all of you sitting out there are now conscious that there is a Higher Power. There is One on whom you can depend.

So I pondered there, after this experience. I thought about the very simple terms on which it had come. I thought about its profound simplicity and yet its deep mystery. For indeed, I did feel released. And it seemed to me that other alcoholics could find a kindred experience.

And I began to sense that one alcoholic talking to another might do what no others could to open the way for the grace of God. So I commenced to work with others. And nothing happened. A succession of failures there was for six months. Meanwhile, my first friend began to stumble and fall by the wayside and would not be picked up and set right.[9]

Bill was referring to his friend Ebby as the one who visited him on Clinton Street and also at the hospital on the day of his spiritual experience. He used the term "released." It seems very significant that Bill didn't use a word like "recovered" or "cured" but "released." In his first use of the word here he said, "A friend of mine who had been released of his obsession by the grace of God."

A few sentences later Bill again used the word and said it this way: "We know that he impressed me because he presented a spectacle of release." While Bill lay in the hospital, Ebby called on him and Bill said, "I asked him once more what the terms of his release were."

In this speech, Bill shared what have since become known as the "original six steps." These six steps were used by the nameless society that became Alcoholics Anonymous in 1939. Bill claimed that these steps came directly from Ebby. The steps an alcoholic needed to take were:

- Admit that he couldn't manage his own life.
- Get honest with himself as never before.
- Make a confession of his character defects.
- Try to sweep away the debris of the past and mend broken relationships with others.
- Experience a new kind of giving that demanded no rewards.
- Accomplish these things by asking God for His help.

It is interesting to note that when Bill W. wrote his story for the book *Alcoholics Anonymous* (the Big Book, published in 1939) he never used the word "release" or "released." Apparently this idea of having been "released" was something that Bill reflected on in later years.

In the Big Book, Bill tells about his last stay in the hospital the following way.

> At the hospital I was separated from alcohol for the last time. Treatment seemed wise, for I showed signs of delirium tremens [DTs]. There I humbly offered myself to God, as I then understood

Him, to do with me as He would. I placed myself unreservedly under His care and direction. I admitted for the first time that of myself I was nothing; that without Him I was lost. I ruthlessly faced my sins and became willing to have my new-found Friend take them away, root and branch. I have not had a drink since.

He continues:

My schoolmate visited me, and I fully acquainted him with my problems and deficiencies. We made a list of people I had hurt or toward whom I felt resentment. I expressed my entire willingness to approach these individuals, admitting my wrong. Never was I to be critical of them. I was to right all such matters to the utmost of my ability. . . .

These were revolutionary and drastic proposals, but the moment I fully accepted them, the effect was electric. There was a sense of victory, followed by such a peace and serenity as I had never known. There was utter confidence. I felt lifted up, as though the great clean wind of a mountain top blew through and through. God comes to most men gradually, but His impact on me was sudden and profound.[10]

In his Big Book recollection Bill doesn't talk about sinking into a depression or being in agony and calling out to God. He seems to focus on different details of the experience.

As Bill got older he attempted to step away from AA, not because he no longer needed the principles or the fellowship, but because he recognized that AA members, and perhaps the AA headquarters, had become too dependent on him. He wanted to continue to help alcoholics but began moving outside of AA to do so. Bill was invited to speak before an assembly of AA doctors in Indianapolis in 1966 about his personal experiences with the vitamin B_3 therapy, which he had undertaken to treat his long-standing depression. He agreed to this invitation only after the committee was able to secure confirmation that Dr. Abram Hoffer, who had worked closely with Bill on the niacin research, would also attend. During a presentation Bill told about his last visit, as a patient, to Towns Hospital.[11]

> The story's old to you, you've read it, I've told you a thousand times the story of my drinking. So I shall quickly bring myself to that day in 1934 midsummer when another physician was speaking. Dear ol' Dr. Silkworth will certainly be known in our annals as a medical saint for so long as AA shall last. Someone once wrote a *Grapevine* piece about him and the title was "The Little Doctor Who Loved Drunks." And from the point of view of the rationalist and the scientific man, the little doctor was a nobody.
>
> He [Dr. Silkworth] said, "Sure there is a lunatic compulsion to drink, certainly, true enough. No doubt it may have psychological causes, trauma in youth, etc. But," he said, "I think there is a big moral question here."
>
> And he also said, "I believe that there is something wrong with the body and the metabolism of alcoholics. For, short of not knowing what it is, I use a widely understood term called 'allergy.' So this adds up to a compulsion that condemns the victim to drink against his will and interest, until the destruction is complete. And this is joined to a physical condition that ensures his lunacy, and finally his demise."
>
> On this hot summer night this dear little man who up to then had worked in drying out joints, and then finally Towns Hospital, where I used to go, with perhaps twenty-five thousand drunks, with occasional successes here and there. He worked on a pittance; he boarded in the place. He had a room upstairs.
>
> As gently as he could, he told Lois what the score was — just like Jung speaking to Rowland.

Author's note: *Bill refers here to Rowland H., who was treated by the famous psychoanalyst Carl Jung by various accounts in 1926, 1930, or 1931, and was pronounced incurable unless he could have a deep spiritual awakening. This is what took him to the Oxford Group, where he had the transformation that he shared with Ebby, who took the message to Bill.*

He [Dr. Silkworth] said, "When Bill came here he clearly wanted so desperately to stop that I thought that he might be one of the few. But I'm afraid that I must say that he isn't! He's beginning to be deteriorated. I am afraid that if he were to remain sane or even live long he will have to be committed."

So this is the sense that science in the persons of Dr. Jung and of Dr. Silkworth passed upon me, upon all of us. Both these truly great men, great human beings had had the courage to say what they believed. . . .

Well, just after leaving the hospital, I had stayed sober for a month or two out of sheer fear, constant vigilance, and then I was in the toils again. About that time Ebby landed in New York and was parked, because he was penniless, in Calvary Mission.

I'm sitting at the kitchen table; Lois is working in that department store. I had a communication — kind of the language of the heart — with the delicatessen which supplied me with gin on credit. And I sat drinking. . . .

So the telephone rang, and here's Ebby. I thought he had gone to the booby hatch. I said, "Come on over. We'll talk about the good old days." Aw, what a very significant line, "the good old days." Today was unbearable, and there would be no future, so we would talk.

He appeared in the doorway, and at once I sensed something indefinably different about him. He came in and we sat at the kitchen table in the basement. On it, I had a big pitcher — full of gin with a little pineapple juice sloshed in so as to suggest cocktails instead of the straight stuff when Lois got home from the store. I set out the tumbler for him and started to pour. He said, "No thanks!"

What? No thanks?! "What's got into you, Ebby? Not drinking?!"

"Not today."

"Well," I said, "Come now, what's happened? Let's have it."

He looked at me and he said, "I've got religion!"

Well, if I'd been deflated by the scientists, this really let me down to the middle of the earth. Because I had had a wonderful scientific education too, just like our last speaker. Well, one must be polite, so I said to Ebby, "What brand is it?"

He said, "I wouldn't exactly call it a brand." And then being very careful to avoid the aggressive evangelism of the Oxford Group, he merely told me his story. How he met Hazard, and had come to New York, and [how] he felt unaccountably released from this desire to drink. Well this "release" was a new one. They were always talking about the water wagon.

His story carried great conviction to me over this identification—no doubt at great depths over which simple ideas could be pitched in. Instead of having to use the corkscrew of the psychiatrist on the top, he was able to see right straight through. He hadn't presented me with a single new idea at all, but I will say that after that conversation I could never be the same man again. Without pressuring me at all, he took his leave.

In no waking hour in the days that followed could the vision of Ebby speaking across the kitchen table leave me. Of course I felt trapped. I said, "If only I could go along with this. Honesty? Yes, you could make a try. Helping other people? Dandy, you know I'm public spirited. But the God bit? No!" And this, although he had played it down, appeared to be the crux of it.

Finally one morning after Lois had gone and I'd got partly tanked up, I said, "I've got to get a clear look at this thing." I arrived up at Towns Hospital half stewed. Dr. Silkworth looked at me sadly. I brandished the bottle and yelled, "Doctor, this time I got something." And the old man said, "I'm afraid you have—you better get upstairs and go to bed."

I wasn't in too bad of shape. The sedatives and that sort of thing were out of me within two or three days. Then suddenly one morning about eleven o'clock Ebby stood in the door. Well, I was glad to see him, but I suspected that this would be the time that he'd turn up the heat on the evangelism. It is said by theologians that prudence is one of the greatest virtues and Ebby had it.

He coyly sat down and we began to talk about the folks up home and this, that, and the other thing until he obliged me to ask him, "What's this little bunch of clichés now—let's see how it was. You admit that you can't run your own life, you get honest with yourself about yourself, you talk it out with somebody — sort of a confession — make restitution for harms done, and then you pray to whatever God there is."

Ebby said, "Yeah, that's about it!" . . . Finally, without exerting one ounce of pressure on me, he got up and went out of there.

I thought to myself, "This fella really practices what he preaches." He had already bound me to him in the cords of a new understanding and love — spoken to me at depths in the language of the heart. We all know what happened; yes, I was prepared for the great event of my life.

After he had gone, I had commenced my old struggle with the "God bit" and I finally thought, "Well, was it the egg that came first, or was it the hen?" And I could not decide; and this brought me down into a depression for which there is no description at all. I mean the sheer hysterical agony of this thing is beyond words. Finally and momentarily, the last vestige of this prideful obstinacy was rubbed out. As a small child frightened by the dark in this strange womb in which I had found myself, I cried out, *"If there is a God, will He show Himself?"*

Instantly the place seemed to light up in a blinding glare. I was instantly transported into an ecstasy beyond description. I began to have visions of the mind's eye, of sort. It seemed to me that I was on a mountain; a great wind was blowing, and it came around me and then passed through me. I thought to myself, "This is not of air, this is of spirit! This is the God of the preachers."

Then the ecstasy subsided a great deal and I found myself lying on that bed; but now I am in a new dimension, just as our late friend put it. "I was a part of the great universe at last." In however small a way, I did belong and I reveled in this. Then at length science came back and said, "My God, you're hallucinating."

So then comes the "little doctor who loves drunks." I had summoned him. I said, "Doc, as well as I can recount it, here it is. This is what has seemed to happen; what I know has happened, and yet I am frightened. Am I hallucinating?"

He questioned me very carefully and very gently and he

finally said great words for Alcoholics Anonymous. Said that obscure little doctor, with no professional reputation, "Bill, some great psychic event has occurred. I don't pretend to understand it. I have read about these things in the books; I know they happen. Now I have witnessed one! And dear boy, whatever it is you better hang onto it. It's so much better than that which had you only an hour ago."

Bill clearly understood the importance of Dr. Silkworth's words and throughout his life he commented on how things might have been different had the doctor dismissed his spiritual experience as a hallucination — or perhaps given him a sedative.

In the same talk Bill spoke of Ebby's returning the following day with a book, *The Varieties of Religious Experience* by William James. He read the book and was deeply moved by the commonality of many of these experiences. Bill went on to say:

Nearly all of these transforming spiritual experiences had a basis of calamity concerning a controlling situation in the life of the individual that on his resources, or on any other resources, could not be transcended. He could not get over, around, or under; and when that got him at depth he was wide open for what we agree with our friends of religion is "God's Grace."

The problem of bringing other alcoholics to this experience was not the problem of bolstering up his ego — it was of deflating it! As a deflationary tool, one thought, "Well, Jung had handed it to Hazard, Ebby handed it to me, but most particularly had Silkworth. In other words, here was my god of science saying, "For you, I can do nothing." So deflation at depth — today we bring on by talking about a compulsion that condemns us to drink coupled with a physical condition that condemns us to lunacy and death.

Over the six months following this experience, Bill went all over New York trying to fix drunks. He would later say that he had a mission to fix all the drunks in the world. He also said that he was prone to grandiosity and his experience had a certain paranoid component. Needless to say, he was unsuccessful in his attempts but managed to stay sober himself — perhaps that being the result of working with others.

chapter three

The Meeting That Changed History

MANY WHO READ THIS CHAPTER will already be familiar with Bill W.'s business venture that took him to Akron, Ohio, in the spring of 1935. This failed business trip ultimately led Bill to his meeting with Dr. Bob. One longtime member of AA recently presented me with this question: "What would have happened if Bill's business trip had been a success?"[12]

Of course, no one could accurately predict the outcome if the business trip had gone the way that Bill wanted. He was hoping to be named president of the company and to finally be back on his feet financially. Clearly he had been frustrated with the reality that his wife was supporting him through her job at the department store and his friends and family were beginning to question if he'd ever get a job.

Alcoholism had robbed Lois and Bill of their friends and business associates. Since sobering up in December 1934, he had spent almost all of his time attempting to help other alcoholics find a spiritual solution similar to his. For the most part, he was still unemployable. This trip to Akron was his first real break since getting sober and surely he was excited at the prospect of employment with a lucrative income.

Certainly many alcoholics coming into AA today can identify at some level with Bill's dilemma. He was newly sober, jobless, and experiencing feelings of limited self-worth and fear of the future. He believed that he could stay sober after his spectacular spiritual experience, but questioned if anyone else would have the same experience. He had tried for nearly six months to help others in New York to get and stay sober with no results.

I'm not sure of the source, but I have heard that Lois lifted Bill's spirits by suggesting that, although he wasn't successful in getting anyone to stay sober, his working with others had been keeping him sober. Also, although Bill couldn't know this at the time, it's a matter of record that some of the people Bill initially worked with later became sober and joined AA.

Shortly before Bill traveled to Akron, he visited with his friend Dr. Silkworth. Bill often spoke of that meeting and Dr. Silkworth's suggestions, which he was able to utilize when he met Dr. Bob for the first time.

In a 1951 speech in Atlanta, after recapping his spiritual experience, Bill shared the story of the events leading up to that visit to Akron, the visit that brought the two men together at the invitation of a woman named Henrietta Seiberling.

4 Well, to me this had come with such mysterious power — yet on such utterly simple terms. Of course I thought, as you would have thought, "Why, every alcoholic should be able to find an experience like this." And then I questioned myself and said, "Well, why didn't these truths hit me this way before? Why of course, 'one alcoholic was talking to another.'" He [Ebby] must have struck me deep; he must have deflated me way down and made room for the grace of God that was forever blocked by my own raging ego. The ability to live in my world, the ability to transmit me, the ability to humble me where no other living one could — that was one alcoholic talking to another.

Maybe that was the clue! If you were in my place, you would have started to work frantically with other alcoholics, and I did — just as many of you have since done, nearly all of you in fact.

I worked with these others and told them of this sudden experience — which incidentally down in New York is called by the cynical "Bill Wilson's Hot Flash." The drunks in those early days weren't a damn bit impressed with that "hot flash" business. They all tapped their heads and said, "NO."

So I worked, and I worked, and I worked; well you know what the defect was, I had become a preacher. I was talking off a moral hilltop. For with this experience came a liability, a certain spiritual pride, a conceit. I fancied I was divinely appointed to fix up all the drunks in the world. Boy, how the drunks knocked that out of me — not one success in six months. About this time Lois's relatives began to murmur, "When is this guy going to stop being a missionary and go back to work?"

Under that gentle prodding I used to go over to Wall Street where I once had been, and I sat around on chairs in brokerage shops, and that made it look to folks like I was working. One day I'm sitting beside a stranger and we fall into a conversation and you know how things can snowball in the streets. All of a sudden it falls into a deal and very suddenly I'm in the midst of a proxy row, and all of a sudden I find I have a controlling interest in a little company and it looks like they're going to elect me president of a little company out in Akron, Ohio. All this rolled up in a matter of a couple weeks resulting from a conversation with a stranger.

On what slender threads this destiny of ours has often hung. So I'm in Akron and I'm going to be elected president of the company. Now we're going to be respectful. We will hold up our heads in this community and when I get the economic situation fixed up — then maybe I'll work some more with these drunks. And we'll get Lois out of that damned department store!

Those were my thoughts. This new crowd threw their proxies on the table, but they didn't have enough so I wasn't president. They took off in the general direction of New York, leaving me broke in the hotel lobby of the Mayflower Akron. With waves of anger and self-pity — fierce anger too because I suspected those proxies had been forged — suddenly I realized I was in danger of getting drunk. And I panicked and alternately I was looking in a bar. It was a Saturday afternoon and that familiar buzz was rising in there. I thought maybe I can scrape up an acquaintance and maybe have a glass of ginger ale. Oh, there started the old rationalization train; but this time I had been restored to sanity. I spotted that typical train of rationalizations and I said, "Hey, look out, you're gonna get drunk — you're gonna get drunk!"

What shall I do? Then came another realization of those other alcoholics; none of them had sobered up, but how often had my anger, and tension, and self-pity disappeared when I had tried to work with them, even without success? Yes, I could lose my life to find it in the life of another. And then I saw that for my own protection I needed another alcoholic as much as he needed me and this was a basic realization.

I sought one out and you know that prodigious chain of circumstance, which could have been nothing but providential. This brought me face to face with Dr. Bob and dear Anne [Dr. Bob's wife] in the living room of a non-alcoholic [Henrietta Seiberling]. One who of a great crowd of people was the only one who seemed to have time enough and seemed to care enough to bring that meeting about. I told Dr. Bob about alcoholism, the malady of my own experience of drinking, of my release, and, frankly, of my present peril. I told him how much I needed him and I think we had begun to get the essentials of it, for something passed between us. Something happened; I think AA began right there, on that June day in 1935.[13]

This speech is another example of Bill's recalling one of AA's most important events and getting the details wrong. This first meeting with Dr. Bob was held at the gatehouse on the estate where Henrietta Seiberling lived — not in her living room — and the date was not in June, but Mother's Day, May 12. It's impossible to know why Bill was occasionally inaccurate with some dates and events. It is possible he was simply trying to move the story along. And with AA recognizing June 10 as the official founding date, it's easy to see how Bill would have used the phrase "on that June day."

As mentioned in the introduction, I will present the same story in different ways, not so much to show the conflicting accounts of history but to provide a different perspective, often where new information is being revealed. For example, in the following speech from 1954, Bill talks about receiving the book *The Varieties of Religious Experience* just after his spiritual experience and before he began working with others. This time, when describing the trip to Akron, he elaborates on some details missing from his earlier recollection.[14]

5   Pretty soon another source comes walking into that hospital in the shape of a book. It was called *The Varieties of Religious Experience* by William James. I think it was then in circulation among the Oxford Groups. I remember how avidly I went through those pages. It was kind of a "learned" document, a little over my head. But out of it stood these common denominators: the people who get these transforming experiences more readily are those who utterly surrender and give up; then the transformation sets in. Sometimes in a blaze, such as mine did, but that doesn't make any difference.

It may take weeks, may take months, but it is a transforming experience that apparently arises out of some terrific collapse at depth. That much stood out of those pages. Then I realized how I had been conditioned for this — the god of science, Dr. Jung, Dr. Silkworth said no! You can't do it on your own resources and you can't do it on the resources of science. Of yourself you are literally nothing. It isn't a question of God's help and you'll do it; you can't do anything! And when we got to that point of complete defeat, when those cases in the book did, then the transformation would set in and would so change and remotivate the people that it couldn't be accounted for by any association or program of discipline.

It had begun to be clear. So I go down to the Oxford Groups and we have here tonight another friend [Sam Shoemaker, rector of the Calvary Episcopal Church] who was a channel for the inspiration that Rowland got, and Ebby got, and I got. It was from him and his living example and the principles he taught that we have drawn the essential elements of our recovery program in AA. In other words, the scientist deflated Ebby, and me, and Rowland and made us ready. Here was the fellow who channeled in the truth which we were then able to buy. He is a great soul and this society will forever be in his debt. He was mightily used as a channel for us, as he has been mightily used in this country and all over the world. So it's about time you knew Sam Shoemaker better; and I'm going to ask him to get up here and reminisce about his first impressions of us drunks as we were trying to get well down around his church.

After Reverend Shoemaker made a few comments, Bill continued with his speech by saying the following.

I was soon heard to say, "I'm going to sober up all the drunks in the world." And we set out to do it. The house over at Clinton Street was filled with drunks. We visited them at Calvary Mission, up at Towns Hospital, anywhere we could lay hands on them, and nothing whatever happened for six months. . . .

Meanwhile I was telling people about this strange experience. I was preaching; I was teaching; I was playing "The Messiah" and nobody would buy it! So one day, pretty crestfallen, I went up to confide in good old Dr. Silkworth. He said, "Look Bill, you've got the cart before the horse. What about this James book? You used to talk about this idea of 'getting deflation at depth.'"

He said, "You're running around talking about this mystic experience of yours and people think you're nuts. No . . . you can identify with these people because you had a drinking experience. You can do it where I can't do it. But then why don't you pour it into them how utterly hopeless, from a medical standpoint, this thing is. The obsession that condemns them to drink against their will and their best interests and the increasing bodily sensitivity that ensures they will go mad or die. Pour that into them and maybe that will soften them up and then they'll buy some of this morality and some of these ideas that will cure them."

About that time people began to murmur, "Why doesn't this guy go to work?" In fact, I think some of my friends got guidance from God that I should go back to work. So I began sitting around Wall Street brokerage houses waiting for something to turn up and it did. Suddenly I'm in the midst of a little proxy row that took me out to Akron, Ohio. Through some quickly found friends, I hoped to get control . . . of a small company and then, of course, this would supply me the living, and in my spare time maybe we'd fix some drunks.

We get to Akron and the deal blows up in my face. My friends depart in disgust and I'm in the Mayflower Hotel with ten dollars in my pocket; not enough for a fare home. For the first time since that experience in Towns Hospital, I began to be afraid. I found myself walking up and down in the Mayflower lobby. It was Saturday afternoon. The barroom was filling up; then I'd ease down to the other end of the corridor and there stood a church directory and absently I kept looking at it.

Suddenly I was seized with a real panic. I said to myself, "Look, you're in a fair way to get drunk." Then I walk up and down again. "Why not go in the barroom and order a bottle of ginger ale. You might scrape up an acquaintance — pretty lonely." Then it occurred to me, in fact it was borne into me for the first time, that even though the effort I had made with other alcoholics had apparently brought nothing to them, it had brought a great deal to me!

Then I see: not teacher, not preacher, not evangelist, no! I need another alcoholic so I can forget my troubles by talking to him. I need him as much as he needs me, and I stopped again before the church directory and ran my finger down the list of churches and preachers. It stopped at the name of Walter Tunks; he turned out to be the Episcopal preacher in town. I called up and I said, "I'm an alcoholic from New York and I'm in a bad way. I am not drunk, but I may get that way; I've got to have another drunk to work on."

This was something of a shock to the good man; drunks one by one were bad enough but not by twos and threes! However, he caught on. He was very nice and gave me a list of some Oxford Group people. The Oxford Group at that stage in Akron had kind of broken up into some factions. Nevertheless, one chap [Norman Shepherd] was very helpful and I finally got a list of maybe ten people.

I began to call them up. It was a Saturday afternoon and people were going away; they couldn't be found — "See you in church Sunday" — until finally I exhausted the whole list. And at the end of the list stood the name "Seiberling." I said, "Uh-oh, this must be the wife of that rubber magnate [F. A. Seiberling, founder of Goodyear Tire and Rubber Company, Henrietta Seiberling's father]. What would she want with a drunk from New York on a Saturday afternoon, looking for a drunk to work on?"

I even went downstairs and looked in the bar again, and something said to me, "You better make that call." And so I did. A lovely southern voice came over the wire and I quickly told her my story. She said, "I'm no alcoholic, but I think I understand. Will you come right straight out here?"

She was another friend who had time and cared enough. I told her the story and she told me about Dr. Bob — how he had fallen apart in that town as a surgeon, how he had tried the groups and read religious literature, how he had tried church attendance, and how he'd been treated medically. She knew he wanted to stop; why couldn't he stop?

She called Smith's house and Anne answered and said, "Well, this sounds interesting, Henrietta, but I don't think we can come over today. You see it's Mother's Day and Bob is a sentimental man, and he has just come home with a great big potted plant for me. And he has set the plant upon the table, but he's so 'potted' that he is on the floor." So Henrietta politely said, "Why don't you come over tomorrow?"

The next afternoon at 5:00 Dr. Bob and Anne walked in the door of Henrietta's house. She discreetly ushered Dr. Bob and me into her library. Dr. Bob said, "I can't stay but a few minutes."

I said, "I know just how you feel, you're shaky, you probably want a drink." The upshot was that we talked for four or five hours. And as his story in the book *Alcoholics Anonymous* will show, and his recording made at Detroit not long before he died further demonstrates, the impression I made upon him was not directly of any spiritual character at all.

He says over and over, "This is the first man that I ever met-up with who knew what he was talking about concerning alcoholism, out of his own experience, and out of the 'mouths of science.'" In other words, I took Silky's advice and I poured the death sentence into him as hard as I could, so far as him being able to get over it by himself. The spark that was to be Alcoholics Anonymous was probably struck then and there.

I went to live with Dr. Bob; Anne thought it would be a little safer. My business continued somehow in Akron for a while and I stayed there during that summer. Pretty soon Dr. Bob was saying to me, "Bill, we better get to work! We better find some drunks."

So he called the City Hospital and got a hold of the head nurse down there. He said there was a man from New York with a cure for alcoholism. The nurse said, "Doctor, have you tried it yourself?" He persisted. She said, "We've got just the man for you. He just came in here, he used to be a city councilman, a well-known lawyer about town, and he couldn't get home from here the last six times. He'd been in there six times in four months; he couldn't even get home sober. We've got him strapped down; he blackened the eyes of one nurse before we did it. How would that one suit you?"

Doctor said, "Well, put him to bed, here's the medication, and we'll be down as soon as he clears up." Presently, Doctor Bob and I looked at the first man on the bed and that was Bill D. who passed out of our sighting only a few weeks ago. He never relapsed since; he kept the faith. Then in Akron, the city on the hill, three candles were lit that stayed lit. How many people then contributed — vital contributions — Doctor Jung, good old Silky, William James, Sam Shoemaker.

Who then invented Alcoholics Anonymous? Well, it was God Almighty. Such is the story of how we alcoholics learned to be free of our obsession. May God grant that this AA trilogy of Recovery, Unity, and Service be a stairway which shall continue so long into the future as God may need us.

Bill always enjoyed telling the story of the Akron meeting, doing so at almost every invitation. But the more taciturn
Dr. Bob also enjoyed sharing his memories of the events when
given the opportunity. In a 1948 talk in Detroit, which fortunately was recorded, Dr. Bob described these early Akron
events.[15]

6   When he came out to Akron on this business mission, which
perhaps for the good of all of us turned out to be quite a flop,
although he had the thing licked but didn't know it, he was
tempted to drink. And he was pacing up and down the lobby
of the Mayflower Hotel wondering whether he better buy those
two fifths of gin and be "king for a night," as he expresses it, or
not. And his teachings led him to believe that he possibly might
avoid getting into difficulties if he found some alcoholic on whom
to work. Spying the name of our good friend Reverend Walter
[Tunks] from the bulletin board in the lobby of the Mayflower, he
called up the good doctor and asked him the names of some of the
group of people [Oxford Group] with whom he had been affiliated
and through whose instrumentality he had acquired sobriety.

The good doctor said he wasn't one, but he knew of quite a
number and he gave him quite a little list; I guess about nine or
ten of them. So Bill starts to call 'em up without very much success. They had either just left town or were just leaving town or
they were having a party or they had a sore toe or something.
Anyway, he came down to the end, or very nearly the end, and
happened to get our good friend, Henrietta.

But he called up good "Henry" and told her what he wanted,
and she said to come right out and have lunch with her. So out he
went, and went into his story in considerable detail and she said,
"I have just the man for you." So she rushes to the phone and
calls up Anne, and tells her she has just the fellow to be helpful to
Bob — we should come over.

Annie said, "Well, I guess we better not go over today." But
Henry is a very persistent, very determined individual. She said,
"Oh, yes, come on over. I know he'd be helpful to Bob."

Well, Annie didn't think this quite wise for us to come over today, and finally Henry bore in to such an extent that she had to tell her that I was very much in the sack and, in fact, had passed all capabilities for listening to any conversation and it would just possibly have to be postponed. So she starts in the next day, having invited us, it being Sunday and Mother's Day. And Anne said that we would be over.

Well, I don't ever remember a feeling much worse. But being very fond of Henry and having said we'd go over, we started over and I extracted the solemn promise from Anne on the way over that fifteen minutes of this stuff was tops, that I didn't want to talk to this "mug" or anybody else, and we'd really make it snappy. Now these are actual facts, that we got there at five o'clock and it was 11:15 when we left.

Now you know, or possibly your memories are good enough to carry you back to certain times when you hadn't felt too good. And you can easily visualize the fact that you wouldn't have listened to anybody, unless that individual had really had something to tell you. And that's the way I felt about Bill, and I recognized the fact that he did have something and so I listened those many hours. And I stopped drinking immediately.

But very shortly after that there was a medical meeting in Atlantic City, and I developed a terrific thirst for knowledge. I had to have knowledge. So I would go to Atlantic City and I would absorb lots of knowledge. I usually mention the fact that I incidentally had acquired a thirst for a scotch, but I didn't mention that. But anyway, I went to Atlantic City and really hung one on and when I came to I was in the home of a friend of ours in Cuyahoga Falls, one of our suburbs. And Bill came over and got me, and got me home, gave me a hooker or two of scotch that night and a bottle of beer the next morning. And that was on the 10th of June of '35 and I have had no alcohol in any form that I know of since.

Now the interesting part of all this, and not all these sordid details, but the condition that we two fellas were in — we had both been associated with the same bunch of people [the Oxford

Group], he in New York and l in Akron. l had been associated, in fact, with them for two years and a half — he for five months. He had acquired this idea of service and l had not. But l had done an immense amount of reading, which they recommended. l had refreshed my memory on the Good Book, and l had had an excellent training in that as a youngster.

They told me that l should go to their meetings regularly and l did, every week. They said l should affiliate myself with some church, and we did that. And they also said that l should cultivate the habit of prayer, and l did that — at least to quite a considerable extent for me. But l got tight every night. And l mean that. It wasn't every once-in-a-while; it was practically every night. And l couldn't understand what was wrong. l had done all these things that these good people had told me to do — every one of them. And l thought very faithfully and sincerely, but l still continued to overindulge.

7 But the one thing that they hadn't told me was the one thing that Bill had: the instruction to attempt to be helpful to somebody else. So we immediately started to look around for prospects and it wasn't long before one appeared in the form of a man whom you all know — at least a great many of you know — our good friend from Akron. Now l knew that this Bill [Bill D., AA number three] was Sunday school superintendent. And l also thought that he'd probably forgotten more about the Good Book every night than l ever knew. And who was l to be telling him about it? And it made me feel somewhat hypocritical. It was quite a job for me to talk to him on that sort of subject. But anyway, we both did, and I'm very glad to say the conversation fell on fertile ground.

My research has revealed that the dates of the American Medical Association Convention in Atlantic City were June 10 through June 14. This information brings into question the accuracy of the date Dr. Bob says he had his last drink. Based on the stories told by Dr. Bob and Bill, it is likely that Dr. Bob's last drink was one week later than he stated.

Of course these conflicting details are not all that surprising when we consider that neither Bill nor Dr. Bob was documenting any of these events for history. They were focusing on staying sober, working with others, and paying their bills. It is important that we remember that alcoholism had caused both cofounders considerable financial burdens.

Dr. Bob's son, Bob Jr., later became a member of Al-Anon. He drove his mother and father over to the gatehouse on Mother's Day, and he always said that Dr. Bob had a terrible hangover and insisted that they only stay fifteen minutes. Bob Jr. (Smitty) told the following about some of the early Akron events.[16]

> Henrietta Seiberling was a friend of my mother's and she called and said, "Anne, there's a man out here who thinks he can help Bob — bring him right on out." Well, my mother had to explain to Henrietta that Bob was in no shape to see anybody, but being good Al-Anon material she'd get him out there the next day.

Author's note: Although Anne Smith dedicated herself to working with alcoholics and their families, she was never a member of Al-Anon. She died in 1949 and Al-Anon officially began in 1951.

> He had a terrible hangover, and finally he said, "Okay, fifteen minutes with this bird is all I want." But when they got there, he and Bill went off into a room by themselves and it wasn't fifteen minutes — they stayed several hours.
>
> As a result of that meeting and at my mother's invitation, Bill came to live in our home there in Akron, Ohio, for all that summer, a three-month period of time. This was the time and the place where Alcoholics Anonymous was first started.
>
> I would like to take some of the time you have allocated to me to tell you about the beginning of some of these movements. I think that they offer a hope and I think they have been guided by a Higher Power, a Heavenly Father, to keep the thing from making terrible mistakes. I think little nudging miracles have kept it growing to what it is today.

Now it started in the middle of the last Great Depression in Akron, which was a one-industry town. The rubber factories were all there: Goodyear, Goodrich, General, Firestone, Seiberling, Miller, and a bunch of others. When people stopped buying automobiles, they stopped needing tires, and the town just fell flat on its face economically. There were strong men on the street corners selling apples for five cents apiece. There were repo cars, just tier after tier stored in the downtown garages. That's how tough the times were there. But maybe God provided that providentially because people had a lot of time on their hands and they could be with each other and I think that was so essential when this little movement was first starting.

We lived in a very modest frame home in Akron and we would have lost that if it hadn't been for the mortgage moratorium declared by President Roosevelt in 1933, whereby people like us who could no longer make their mortgage payments were allowed to stay in the home and not be thrown out in the street. Alcoholism and the times had reduced us to a state of absolute poverty. There were times when there was nothing to eat in the house except bread and milk, and sometimes nothing but potato soup. We didn't starve, but at times it was a near thing; it was really an unlikely start.

Echoing Smitty's description of the hard economic times in Akron in the late 1930s is this excerpt from a letter by the wife of an early Akron member. (More such rare letters are found in my book *We Recovered Too.*)

> *Those were days when with many people at the table we might have 11 kinds of potato salad, because we were all too poor to buy wieners. Everyone brought food. I wonder if A.A.s today appreciate how pitifully poor most of us were in those early struggling days.*
> — *Dorothy*[17]

During the summer of 1935, both cofounders worked tirelessly to maintain their own sobriety while trying to help others. As previously mentioned, Bill had attended meetings of the Oxford Group in New York for six months and Dr. Bob in Akron for two and a half years. No doubt the influences of the Oxford Group, a non-denominational Christian fellowship, were helping them to stay sober. Oxford Groups claimed no membership requirements, much like AA today — all who wanted to change their lives were welcome.

One can imagine the conversations in the Smith home, late at night, between Bill W. and Dr. Bob and the morning meditations with Anne Smith by the fireplace. Many of AA's principles were born in Akron that summer.

In late June 1954 Bill W. was invited back to Akron for AA's nineteenth founders celebration. He gave an inspiring talk that detailed much of the early Akron events.[18]

> We are gathered here to commemorate the striking of a spark. A spark that was to light a candle. A candle which at first flickered fitfully and at times nearly went out. But which was then passed from hand to hand until it has reached nearly every distant shore of the world.
>
> I suppose an occasion of this sort would best be served by telling some yarn. Perhaps we would like to think again together about the chains and providential events which led to the striking of this spark over in Henrietta Seiberling's living room nineteen years ago. We then might witness together — and many of you indeed can relive the experience when the spark lit the candle — and we can remember together with gratitude and joy the flying-blind period of our primary time.
>
> And when we have drawn on this at good length, because this is the thing that concerns us most, we might get on the magic carpet, so to speak, and travel worldwide and see how the candle has gone from hand to hand. And then we might presume to lift the veil that obscures our future and wonder what destiny God may have in store for us.
>
> Relative to the events that led up to the striking of the spark, I suppose that humanly speaking, the first man who had anything

to do with this society is one who still does not know that he did. He is none other than Carl Jung, the great pioneer of psychiatry in Zurich, Switzerland. And there, probably in the very early thirties, he had treated a drunk [Rowland H.] for a year. The man had great hope and earnestness to get well. He thought he had got well and then, as he so well understood, found himself, in spite of all these resources, drunk again.

So he goes back to the doctor and says, "How bad is it, Doctor, in my case?" And that very great and humble man, this man of the science of the mind, replied, "Well, Rowland, I have never seen one single case of alcoholism so great as yours that has ever recovered excepting through a religious conversion experience. These experiences, indeed, take on many forms but they all have the same subject. They enable people to do, as by a gift from somewhere, the things that they could not do before. But these events in the world of the alcoholic are only very occasional. Lightning strikes here, it strikes there, we don't know just why."

So our friend Rowland began to search for just such an experience and he found it in the Oxford Movement, then flourishing in the United States and even more so in Europe. He had a summer place near Bennington, Vermont. He heard of the dilemma of a friend of mine [Ebby T.] to be brought before a judge to be committed to an asylum — an old school friend that I hadn't seen in years. He and others of the Oxford Group went to my friend and told him of their own release from drinking. You see here, that early, alcoholics were talking to other alcoholics. It so fell out that my old friend never quite made the grade until very recently, by the way. But the essential ideas were beginning to fall into place.

And that friend came to New York City, and hearing of my plight — that a good doctor said I couldn't live another year — came to see me at 182 Clinton Street, Brooklyn. And across the kitchen table he presented me what are the essential legacies that we now enjoy in this society. He presented me an opportunity to be sober if I would. He presented me much more. He presented me an opportunity to be whole and to be a growing human consumption.

He presented to me, who had then begun to live on borrowed time, an opportunity to serve for many years, to carry this message to others. So the elements of Recovery, Unity, and Service were all contained in that little conversation across the kitchen table. It is the essence of our inheritance.

Well, I was going through my own experience. Most of you know it: how I was released from alcoholism in Towns Hospital in December 1934; how I became possessed of a desire to work with other alcoholics and worked like the dickens for six months. Nothing happened. People began to say, "Well, when is this guy going to quit being a missionary?"

I tried to get into a business deal, finally fell into a rather lame one. It takes me here to Akron and then the deal falls through. And I'm walking up and down the morning after, a Saturday. My friends are gone; I'm by myself, no carfare home. For the first time since my experience six months before, I began to be frightened I would get drunk.

I looked in the bar down there and then I walked to the other end of the lobby and I saw a board on which there were the names of churches and preachers, and by now I said, "Well, I must find another drunk." Not this time to preach to him; not this time to teach him, but because I need his company to keep me sober, which was a marked step in humility for me. I need another drunk by whom I can stay alive myself. For I had found that in working the six months before with a great many alcoholics indeed, that though none of them had dried up, it had a tremendous effect and helpfulness in keeping me sober.

So now the temptation was upon me. I must lose my life to find it in working with somebody else. So I called up a well-loved preacher in this town, Dr. Tunks. (I asked for him today. I said I'd written a letter to his former church. I wondered if it reached him. The good clergyman said to me, "Reach me? All you've got to do is write a letter to Walter Tunks, Ohio, and it'll get to me.")

Anyhow, I announced to the good man over the phone what my need was, that I needed a drunk to work upon. Well, he was a little astounded, he said. I imagine at that time drunks separately were bad enough, but if you began to collect them together, you could have trouble.

But he caught the idea. He referred me to Norman Shepherd, then in the Oxford Group, working at the Firestone Company. Norman gave me a list of people and I canvassed that list eagerly, but everybody seemed to be going somewhere else. They would see me the next day, perhaps. They were cordial, they were nice. Some of them really understood, I think, but nobody could see me then and it was then that I needed help. And at the very end of that list was the name of a person who was to be the link between me and Dr. Bob — who because on that day she cared enough and understood enough we, all of us here, are alive.

The name is Henrietta Seiberling, and I thought it might be some older member of the family and I couldn't imagine going out to one of the Seiberlings on a Saturday afternoon looking for a drunk to work on. It didn't square up.

I even went back downstairs, took another look at the bar-room, another look at the church directory. Something said, "My boy, you'd better make that call." So I made it, and Henrietta's delightful southern voice came on the wire and instantly she caught my need and she said, "Won't you come right out?"

So I land in the gatehouse out there at the Seiberling estate and met Henrietta, who so many of you know and love. She took me in there and we talked a little while and she said, "I know just the one for you. That would be Dr. Bob. Oh, that fellow has tried so hard, but somehow he can't seem to do it. I'm sure you'll help him." [This conversation took place on a Saturday, but Bill describes it as Sunday, Mother's Day.]

8 She goes immediately to the phone. It's Mother's Day. She calls up over there and Anne answers. And Henrietta says, "There's a man from New York who says he's an alcoholic, whatever that is, and I think he can help Dr. Bob."

Anne said, "Why perhaps he can, but not just at the moment, Henrietta, because it is Mother's Day, you know, and Dr. Bob is a sentimental dear. And he has just come in with a potted plant for me which he has placed on a table, but he is so 'potted' that he is under the table. I don't think we'll be over."

But said Henrietta lightly, as one who understood and cared enough, "But Anne, can't you come over tomorrow?"

"Well," Anne said, "We'll try and bring him."

Henrietta said to me, "Take dinner with me tomorrow and we'll see if we can get them over."

I think it was about five o'clock in the afternoon of that Sunday that Anne and Dr. Bob walked in. Doctor was very restless; he said he couldn't stay, only about five minutes. And as soon as I got him aside, I said, "I understand, old boy, you're pretty thirsty. I don't want to keep you long." But Henrietta discreetly led us into the library just as you come into the door there. We shut the door and began to talk and we kept talking until eleven o'clock at night.

There, I think, something passed between us and the spark was struck. If you look at Dr. Bob's story in the book *Alcoholics Anonymous,* you will see that he was not very much impressed with my spiritual qualifications. And if that were so, he was quite right about it. I never have made too much headway myself. But he was impressed by the fact that I was an alcoholic who had suffered his agonies, knew every twist and turn of his warped mind, and moreover, even though he was a doctor, I was able to bring him medical knowledge of alcoholism, showing him how it was an obsession. Once a habit, but now an obsession that condemned him to drink against his will — and a physical sensitivity that guaranteed that he was to die or go mad if the drinking went on.

Such was the age-old dilemma of the drunk. Time out of mind, and Bob understood and I suppose that struck him at depth, for you see I had stopped talking then about my spiritual qualifications and my white light experience and all that kind of business. In fact, old Doc Silkworth says, "My friend, you've got the cart before the horse. You gotta punch it into these drunks that they're fatally ill, and coming from you it may strike deep enough to soften them up."

If you read Dr. Bob's story, you see that is the essence of the impression that I made on him that day. Well, he did sober up and departed from us in 1950. The "prince of all Twelve Steppers," my most beloved friend, with whom I could say there was never an angry argument or hard word in all our association. And that is a tribute to him and not to me because I had lots of hard words with lots of people but never with Dr. Bob.

Well, Annie was a prudent person and you know that prudence ranks high in the list of Christian virtues. She thought to herself, "Well now, if I invite this fellow Bill to the house, he can kind of keep an eye on Bob. In fact, they might be able to keep an eye on each other."

I wanted to carry on this little proxy fracas I was in; a little lawsuit was going. So I go over to live in the Smith household and never can I forget those early mornings there: Anne sitting by the fireplace; our quiet time; reading from the Bible; Corinthians — that greatest of all definitions of love; and [the New Testament writer] James who said, "Faith without works is dead."

Although much of the same story has been repeated here, I added Bill's comments at the nineteenth Founders Day because he talked a bit more openly. He even mentioned Norman Shepherd as the one name he received from Dr. Walter Tunks. Shepherd led him to Henrietta who led him to the meeting with Dr. Bob.

chapter four

"The Prince of All Twelve Steppers"

SOME PEOPLE HAVE WONDERED, "What exactly was Dr. Bob's contribution to AA?" Of course, he lived only fifteen years after finding his sobriety. Bill was the primary author of the book *Alcoholics Anonymous,* and he authored the Twelve Steps. Bill also wrote more than one hundred *Grapevine* articles, authored the books *Twelve Steps and Twelve Traditions* and *Alcoholics Anonymous Comes of Age,* created the Twelve Concepts for World Service, and wrote the AA Service Manual. There is absolutely no question about Bill W.'s contributions to AA, since the list goes on and on. But how about Dr. Bob: what did he bring to AA as a founder?

I recently had the opportunity to speak with Tom W., a former *Grapevine* editor, AA historian, and personal friend of Bill W. Tom made a comment that really caused me to reevaluate some of my original thoughts about Dr. Bob's role in AA. Tom said, "Dr. Bob lived by the principles of the AA program." [19] He wasn't saying that Bill W. didn't; he was simply stating that in his opinion Dr. Bob was an excellent example of all that is AA.

This motivated me to dig a little deeper to see if I could further answer the question about Dr. Bob's contributions. I began talking with AA members with many years of sobriety who were interested in AA history about Dr. Bob's contributions. Two comments seemed to recur each time I posed the question. One was, "He provided medical care to thousands of alcoholics for no charge." The second was, "He was the steady figure in Bill W.'s life that helped keep Bill from getting too far off course."

I would agree that both of these examples are true, at least to some extent, and I would also say that there was much more to Dr. Bob and his influence on AA and Bill W. For example, Tom W. made the statement that Dr. Bob lived the AA program for fifteen years. Well, what does that look like? One of Dr. Bob's earliest contributions occurred in the summer of 1935 while Bill W. was living with the Smiths. Dr. Bob said to Bill, "Don't you think we ought to be working with some drunks?"

At Founders Day in June 1954, Bill referred to Dr. Bob as the "prince of all Twelve Steppers" and talked about his contributions. Bill shared these words that summer day in Akron.

> Suddenly, that latter phrase began to burn into Bob's consciousness because he said, "Hadn't we better be doing a little Twelve Step work?" So we shopped around at first. There was a preacher down the street; he had one in tow. He's right here today and it wasn't Bill, AA number 3, who was so sick. It was another one, Eddie (and his wife Ruth and the kids). Eddie wasn't ready. He was awfully badly derailed. Anne invited the whole family to come and live there — and how we worked with Eddie and it was a bust.
>
> And long about this time Dr. Bob said, "I gotta go to a convention in Atlantic City."
>
> And Anne made frantic motions to me, "No, no, no." And well, Bob said, "Well, I've always gone; if I miss one of these — or could I, or should I?"
>
> "Well," I said, "After all, you've gotta live in a world where grog is, so why don't you go?" This is about maybe two weeks after the conversation at Henrietta's. So the dear old boy started for the convention. We didn't hear from him for quite a while for some reason or other. And about four o'clock in the morning

on the fifth day, he got poured off the train and went over to the house of his nurse, where we, Annie and I, found him.

It was a terrible dilemma then. Not only the alcoholic dilemma, but there was a certain surgical dilemma. About three days hence, an operation had to be performed by him on some-body — and a serious one.

When he realized the plight he was in, and the frightful hangover he had, well it was something serious. So we started an around-the-clock tapering operation on the old boy. And the idea, you see, was to edge him up to that operation, not too tight to do it, but not so sober that he couldn't. On the third night of this pro-cess in which we got him eased down off the perch, Anne put Bob and me in the same room. And he was awake at about four o'clock the morning of the operation, and he turned and looked at me, and he said, "Bill, I'm going to go through with it."

I said, "You mean the operation?"

"Oh, yes," he said, "the operation to be sure. No," he said, "what we've been talking about." Smithy was a man of few words, quite unlike me. So he goes down there and I remember how Anne and I waited and prayed while he went into that hospital, and we had him just right. Not too tight, just right, and he did it and he came out of there, and that was June 10, 1935.[20]

Bill mentions Eddie in this talk as the first drunk he and Dr. Bob tried to help. Dr. Bob's son, Smitty, would often tell the story of Eddie, and it seems proper to include Smitty's version of events here.

Bill and Dr. Bob only had two things going for them that I know of. They had an open spiritual mind and the desire for service. So the first thing they set out to find was another alcoholic. And they found a young guy by the name of Eddie R. He had just been thrown out in the street for non-payment of rent with his cute little blonde wife and two kids. So they decided to move the whole shebang into our home. They locked Eddie upstairs in the bed-room where he'd be available as they got this knowledge. You've got to remember that there's nothing written, and they're just staying a page ahead of Eddie.

But Eddie was an agile guy and we had downspouts. And Eddie would open the second-story window and slide down the downspouts and escape. And they'd have to postpone Eddie's treatment to recapture him. One time Eddie got as far as Cleveland, Ohio, which was thirty-five miles away, and called them up on the phone, collect, to let them know he was going to commit suicide. But he would give them time to drive up and witness the event. Can you imagine a more improbable start of anything?

They brought Eddie back and when he sobered up he had a few things that hadn't shown up immediately. And he began beating up on his little blonde wife; and then he began chasing my mother around the house with a butcher knife. So we held a "group conscience meeting" and it was decided that the only thing to do with Eddie was for his little wife to take him back to Ann Arbor, Michigan, and recommit him into a mental institution.

Of course, both Bill and Dr. Bob were crestfallen, because here was their first attempt to sober up another alcoholic together and it was a total failure.

But I want to tell you something. At my father's funeral in 1950, fifteen years later, a man walked up to me and said, "Do you know me?"

And I said, "Yeah, you're Eddie!"

He said, "That's right, and I'm a member of the Youngstown, Ohio, AA group and I've been sober one year!" I tell you this because you never know the result of that Twelve Step call.[21]

Several years ago I had the privilege of viewing some correspondence between Eddie R. and Bill W., exchanged while Bill was writing *Alcoholics Anonymous Comes of Age*. Bill had sent out some manuscript copies to early members asking for their comments and inquiring whether he had the facts correct. In a reply letter, Eddie told Bill that the incident with the butcher knife was overstated and reminded Bill that when he (Bill W.)

and Dr. Bob called on Bill D. (AA number three) at Akron City Hospital, Eddie was with them.[22]

Right from the very beginning, AA members opened up their homes to those they were attempting to help. Dr. Bob and his wife, Anne, continued to invite alcoholics to live in their home. Recently, I saw a list compiled by several historians documenting the early growth of AA. The list included the member's name, sobriety date, and the city in which he lived. I found this list to be very revealing; it also helps to demonstrate the effectiveness of the work being done in Akron in AA's pioneering days.

According to this list (excluding Dr. Bob and Bill W.), thirty-five of the first fifty AA members came from Akron and five from Cleveland. In other words, forty of the first fifty pioneers of AA were either sponsored by Dr. Bob or, at a minimum, strongly influenced by him and Anne.

One of the names on the list was Earl T. Earl was actually from Chicago, but he sobered up in Dr. Bob's home. He later went on to start AA in Chicago. Earl's story in the Big Book (added in its second edition in 1955) gives details of his Akron experience.

> Then and then only, after a thorough indoctrination by eight or nine individuals, was I allowed to attend my first meeting. This first meeting was held in the living room of a home and was led by Bill D., the first man that Bill W. and Dr. Bob had worked with successfully.
>
> The meeting consisted of perhaps eight or nine alcoholics and seven or eight wives. It was different from the meetings now held. The big A.A. book had not been written, and there was no literature except various religious pamphlets. The program was carried on entirely by word of mouth.
>
> The meeting lasted an hour and closed with the Lord's Prayer. After it was closed, we all retired to the kitchen and had coffee and doughnuts and more discussion until the small hours of the morning.

I was terribly impressed by this meeting and the quality of happiness these men displayed, despite their lack of material means. In this small group, during the Depression, there was no one who was not hard up.

I stayed in Akron two or three weeks on my initial trip trying to absorb as much of the program and philosophy as possible. I spent a great deal of time with Dr. Bob, whenever he had the time to spare, and in the homes of two or three other people, trying to see how the family lived the program. Every evening we would meet at the home of one of the members and have coffee and doughnuts and spend a social evening.

The day before I was due to go back to Chicago — it was Dr. Bob's afternoon off — he had me to the office and we spent three or four hours formally going through the Six-Step program as it was at that time. The six steps were:

1. Complete deflation.
2. Dependence and guidance from a Higher Power.
3. Moral inventory.
4. Confession.
5. Restitution.
6. Continued work with other alcoholics.

Dr. Bob led me through all of these steps. At the moral inventory, he brought up several of my bad personality traits or character defects, such as selfishness, conceit, jealousy, carelessness, intolerance, ill-temper, sarcasm, and resentments. We went over these at great length, and then he finally asked me if I wanted these defects of character removed. When I said yes, we both knelt at his desk and prayed, each of us asking to have these defects taken away.[23]

Earl T.'s recollections certainly validate Bill W.'s comment about Dr. Bob's having been the "prince of all Twelve Steppers." If we look at other examples of early AA members who came in through the Akron group, we will clearly hear Earl's experience echoed many times over.

Another early member was Clarence S. of Cleveland. Clarence, who was also sponsored by Dr. Bob, went on to become one of AA's best examples of sponsorship. When invited to speak, Clarence enjoyed talking about those early days with his sponsor. (In this story, Clarence is likely telling about his wife.)

> She told me about this doctor in Akron, Ohio, and asked me if I'd like to go down and meet him. What could I lose? Of course I'd love to meet him. So she bought me a one-way bus ticket to Akron and she put me on it and sent me down there to see Dr. Bob. Now, this was my meeting with my sponsor and I would like to say that I listened to him attentively and ate it all up when he talked to me. But I can't tell you that, because he scared the life out of me and I ran out on him. He knew too much about me.

Later in the same speech Clarence discusses his next visit with Dr. Bob and how he was introduced to the then-nameless fellowship.

> **9** Doc put me in Akron City Hospital and I was in there for I think a week. I remember that I was so sick and so shot that I wasn't even eating at the end of this week. When I left I hadn't starting eating yet; we knew nothing about vitamins yet.
>
> Doc had these men come see me. Every day these fellas would come that were from the Oxford Group there and talk to me; these were the rummies. There were eighteen of them come to see me and I know that because they wrote their names on a sheet; I still have it as one of my relics. They told me the stories of their lives and what had happened to them.
>
> They were all older men, ten, fifteen, twenty years older than me. All of them had really been around and had been through the wringer. They told me what had happened as far as their drinking was concerned and they all told me they had the answer to my problem. But none of them would tell me what this answer was.

The last day I was in this hospital — I can still remember — this is why I know I still wasn't eating, because Paul S. — he's dead and gone by now — some of you folks probably knew Paul — he came in at breakfast time and stayed all day. He ate my breakfast for me and he ate my lunch for me; I did get the dessert.

Author's note: Paul S. was one of the first ten Akron AA members. His story "Truth Freed Me!" appeared in the first edition of the Big Book.

At about four o'clock in the afternoon, Doc came in and he sat on the foot of my bed — a very unprofessional posture. He sat there looking at me a couple of minutes and he said, "Young Fella." (He always had a name for everyone and mine to him was "Young Fella" because I was the young one then; I was only about thirty-five at the time. That was young in those days, but it isn't now; there are a lot of people who come in much younger.)

He said, "What do you think of all this by now?"

I said, "I think this is wonderful — all these fellas coming in to see me. And they're telling me the stories of their lives and all this sort of thing and I don't know them . . . it's wonderful! They all tell me that they have the answer to my problem, but none of them has given me the answer. What is it? What do I have to do? What's the gimmick?"

You see when I went into the hospital I didn't know what it was going to be. I didn't know what the treatment was that I was supposed to get. This was a medical doctor and I was expecting some medical performance. . . . But I didn't have any medicine; they didn't give me anything. I just shook. I didn't even take the whiskey they offered me. I shook this out.

So he said, "We're not too sure about you. You're pretty young and we haven't had any success with these young fellas. They're all screwballs and we don't know for sure that you're ready yet."

I said, "What's to be ready?" I weighed 130 pounds. I had no home, no job, no clothes, no dough, no nothing! I had been whipped. I'd been on the bum for a long time — what do you have to do to be ready?

. . . I had to convince him that I wanted this thing more than anything else. Finally, he must have been convinced and he said, "Okay, I'll tell you what the secret of this is." So I lay back waiting for this big enfoldment here and he points his big bony finger at me. (And he had them big fingers, about this long. He was a big, long gangly fella and those of you that have had the privilege of meeting Doc know that. And he could look right through you.)

He said, "Young Fella, do you believe in God?" I thought, "Holy smokes, I didn't expect anything like that! This is no medicine!" And I'm afraid of anything like this because I had been in missions before and I had been mixed up with these screwballs. I wanted no part of this.

But here I am. I'd been in this hospital a week and I'm under obligation to a bunch of religious nuts. This is what's going through my mind — I'm not saying this — and he's waiting for an answer. So he said, "Well, do you or don't you?"

I said, "Well, I guess I do."

And he said, "There's no guessing about it — either you do or you don't!" This was the soft approach to the spiritual foundation. (Comment made in joking!)

. . . I asked him, "What does that have to do with it?"

He said, "Young Fella, that has everything to do with it!"

And then he asked me this question about believing in God, and I said, "I do."

He said, "Okay, now we can get someplace."

So I thought, "Okay, now we're gonna get some place."

And he says, "Now we'll pray."

I said, "Who will pray?"

He said, "You will."

"I don't know anything about praying."

. . . He said, "I don't suppose you do know anything about praying. All you have to do is repeat after me and that will suffice for this time." So he uttered some prayer and I followed it and felt like a fool, but it didn't kill me. I survived it and I'm glad I did. He shook hands with me after it and said, "Young Fella, you're going to be all right!" So that evening he carried me off to a meeting, and that was my beginning in this fellowship.[24]

Clarence makes the point later in his talk that this early beginning was the "Oxford Group" and that AA was still nameless. His sobriety date was February 1938, and it was around this time that Bill W. and the group in New York began to distance themselves from the Oxford Group. The Akron group was meeting every Wednesday evening in the home of T. Henry and Clarace Williams, who were non-alcoholic members of the Oxford Group; however, many of the early alcoholic members talk about getting together every night in members' homes.

Bill D. of Akron was the first person to successfully get and stay sober as the result of Dr. Bob and Bill W.'s Twelve Step call. He remained sober until his death in September 1954. Bill D.'s story didn't appear in the first edition of the Big Book. I've heard various reasons for this, but I'm uncertain of which is true. However, Bill W. was able to get a recorded interview and included Bill D.'s story in the second edition, which was released ten months after Bill D. passed away.

During the 1940s and early 1950s the idea of tape recording AA meetings hadn't yet caught on. Unfortunately, those recordings that were made and have survived over the years are often very poor quality. I was able to locate one recording of Bill D. on an old reel in the Recovery Speakers Research Center. Here are his comments regarding the early Akron meetings.

> In my opinion, there isn't anything much that helps a person more than leading a meeting. The fact is that it is one of the things they had in mind when we started out. When we went to a meeting in the early days, we didn't know who was going to lead the meeting. We had what we called "quiet time" and during that time we were to open our minds for instruction as to who we thought ought to lead the meeting that night. Then after we sat there in silence for five minutes, we'd go around and see who had the most ["votes"]. We pointed to him and said, "Well, it's you."

In the same speech, Bill D. reflects on being in the hospital and talking with his wife about "these men" that had found an answer. Up until that time the people who had been trying to help him had been from the church, but Bill W. and Dr. Bob had a different story. Here's how Bill D. described the event.

She told me, "They're a couple of drunks like you are; and they've had trouble too and they're trying to quit." They're poor, weak sinners. She didn't say that, but that changed my mind. All these other people around here have come around to help the poor, weak sinner — me. They're all right, but they want to help me. There's nothing wrong with them. But now there's a couple of "poor, weak sinners" that are coming to talk to me.

Well, that helped my egotism quite a bit. They admitted that they had had just the same licking as I had. Others had sort of looked down on me, "Why don't you use your willpower?" Now, I've used my willpower, and so have you, because when you get sober you have a hell of a fight to put on. If I had sense enough, I would have fought that first drink; it would be easier than after I had been out there for a week or two. But finally I knew that I had to quit, so I'd sit there and fight it out. That's when you've got a real tough fight to put out, and I knew my preacher had never gone through that — sick at night in bed, shaking and fighting that out to get sober. I used to always tell them that getting drunk was fun, but not getting sober; that's when my problems started.

But these fellows had the same weakness that I had and I knew it wasn't going to hurt too much to listen to them. They were down on my level. Then there was one other thing that she said, "You're gonna quit!" And that helped a lot and I didn't forget it. I thanked her for the confidence, for I didn't have much confidence. But she went on and I talked about the "Keeley Cure" and all that stuff that I had with my doctor. I had a regular doctor that had been helping me for two or three years, and he was a mighty nice fella and he was a minister too. My wife and I had talked with him about taking "The Cure." And he said, "That won't do Bill any good. He's a confirmed drunkard." That's what he called it.

He said, "I'm a minister and l am a doctor and l ought to have some answer, but l don't have any answer. All in the world l can do is help him through his pain so he can get sober enough to get back to try and stay sober a few days. But that won't work and it won't be long and he'll be calling me again. l know it because l've had them before, but he was a good friend of mine."

So then l asked, "What are they going to charge me?" And l never forgot that answer.

Now we've both been church members for a long time and I'm not knocking the church. We had been constantly going. Now l didn't go too regular, because l would get drunk too often. But when l was sobering up . . . l went pretty drunk sometimes to church.

And she said, "That's the strange thing about this. They said, 'not only were they not going to charge anything, but you couldn't pay them a cent — if you had a million dollars!'"

There's another thing in AA and I'm not going to preach to you. You go out and handle AA your way; I'm not gonna tell you, because if you don't get it right and you get drunk it's going to be you that's sick, not me. I'll sympathize with you, but I'd rather it be you and not me because l don't want to try it anymore. l had enough. That they wouldn't take a cent for the work [Twelve Step work] if you had a million dollars — you couldn't pay them for it — that's the way AA started out.[25]

There is a consistency to the stories of the early Akron and Cleveland members regarding how seriously the individual wanted to stop drinking. Repeatedly, each one described having his ego deflated and having to ask for help. The other constant that comes across strongly is the surrender to and the willingness to accept God. This is not surprising when we keep in mind that AA was still a nameless society and that much of the early influence was coming directly from the Oxford Group and daily Bible study.

Since Bill D. never had the chance to see his Big Book story in print, it is impossible for anyone to know whether or not he agreed with all of the contents. We can, however, see how he and all of these early Ohio members were influenced by Dr. Bob. Unquestionably, most of the early members and groups came out of the work being done in Akron by Dr. Bob and his wife, Anne.

In addition to the people already mentioned, Paul S. and Dick S., Ernie G. (who was AA member four and married Dr. Bob's adopted daughter, Sue), and a host of others got sober as a result of Dr. Bob's work and went on to become major contributors to AA's pioneering times. Another early member worth mentioning is Archie T. of Grosse Pointe, Michigan, who lived with Dr. Bob and Anne for close to a year before moving back home to start an AA group. His story appeared in the first edition of the Big Book, titled "The Fearful One." This excerpt from a talk given by Bob S. Jr. (Smitty) mentions Archie's living with Dr. Bob and his family.

> Some stayed for months and were accepted as part of the family. Archie was with us over a year. They shared in what we had and Mother was their daytime mentor. Her serenity among these circumstances bred serenity among the alcoholics. Her counseling was done quietly and selflessly. She never lost faith in these guys. Of course, she was the one who was cooking the meals, making the beds, and cleaning up the messes. She was also the one on the telephone answering the inquiries as the word began to trickle out.
>
> She made everyone who stayed there have a quiet time in the morning when they might feel nearer to God. This was a requirement which involved some reading of the Bible and study. It was one of her rules.[26]

When documenting Dr. Bob's contributions, it's important to include his life partner, Anne, who was lovingly called the "mother of the first AA group" by Bill W. I believe a case can be made to consider Anne as a founder of AA and/or Al-Anon. After Anne died in 1949, Bill W. asked the early AAs and their wives to comment on Anne. Many responded with wonderful letters of praise acknowledging her love and support. One of those letters, in particular, reveals more about the miracles that were taking place in Dr. Bob and Anne's home.

In the days when no one could afford a hospital, in the days when her own kitchen was a battlefield where with prayer and hot coffee and good fellowship and still more hot coffee, a soul was encouraged to go forth and make a fresh stand against liquor, "because this time you're not alone," Anne was the chief against despondency and despair.

Think back now to those struggling days of 1935. Bill and Dr. Bob and some others would probably tell you that for a time Anne literally was Alcoholics Anonymous. The transition from family group to national organization was in vast degree her accomplishment.

She knew what was "the right thing to do" and had the courage to do it. Intuitively, she began to set up each new convert as a friend, and yet as a separate and distinct unit. People write of her now as if, though departed, she still is with them. That was Anne's special message. "Carry God in your heart. Walk where you will walk with the knowledge that your friends are near you," she counseled. She planted self-confidence in people's hearts and imparted the secret of her own unquestioning faith. It is a reservoir of hope that those who use it find adequate and never-failing.

As with the young man [Archie T.] from a distant city who lived for ten months in the Smith home. "At first I knew in my heart that nothing would ever persuade me to go back to my home city," he writes. "After six months with Dr. Bob and Anne I realized I must go back to the same place where I had fouled up. Anne didn't tell me so. She helped me see myself in the right light so the decision came to me slowly and naturally." Let us add permanently.

Sometimes the miracle that Anne affected took place more simply. A handshake at an A.A. meeting, an introduction to various friends, perhaps a visit to the home — no one kept any count. Anne did no preaching, but she sometimes wrapped everything up in a neat package. "People have been good to you here," she told one. "Be sure that you go out of your way to extend a welcome to newcomers whenever you meet them."

People speak of her knowing how to say the right thing in just the right way. To a newcomer, case-hardened, fearful of facing embarrassment, negative in her thinking, because she has seen her drinking husband "reformed" before and was dubious about the whole thing she said merely, "We are all here for the same purpose. Everything will be alright." And everything was alright.

But it was in the greater and still unknown field of the human soul that Anne Smith effected her works. From that fateful day in 1935 when A.A. took shape in the persons of Bill W. and Dr. Bob, both uncertain as to what each could do for himself but both determined to make a man of the other, she saw her field of usefulness and seized it. No man or woman is powerful enough to defeat alcoholism unaided, but any sincere alcoholic can help rescue some other alcoholic, and in the saving win himself freedom. That was the program, and with God's aid and her husband's tremendous power — he was and is a big man, a man of deep voice and greatness of spirit — she set herself to extend this program to reach thousands who asked to be freed from the slavery of drink.

Truly her soul goes marching on.

— F.B.B.[27]

This letter captures the essence of the love that Dr. Bob and Anne shared with so many people during the years they were ministering to the hopeless in their Akron home and community. Recall my friend Tom W.'s comment that Dr. Bob lived the AA program.[28] A visitor to King School on meeting night would see a tall man wearing glasses and a sweater sitting in the second row. That was Dr. Bob.

Author's note: *The early group of recovering alcoholics met in Dr. Bob and Anne's living room for several months before moving to King School at the beginning of 1940.*

A great deal is said about Dr. Bob's strong, fatherly influence on Bill. Bill accepted Dr. Bob's counsel, respected his judgment, and admired his demonstration of spiritual principles. Of course, Dr. Bob the "prince of all Twelve Steppers" was equally fond of Bill. Published by Alcoholics Anonymous World Services, the book *Dr. Bob and the Good Oldtimers* includes this depiction of their relationship.

> *Both were complex individuals — yet able to express profound ideas in a simple way — and there are probably more reasons than we can ever fathom for this ability they had to work together. Love certainly had something to do with it. Loyalty was another ingredient as far as Bob was concerned. It has been said that he found it hard to refuse Bill, his sponsor, anything. Each wanted to agree with the other and was therefore flexible. There was also a good deal of practical thinking involved. As "co-founders," both were shrewd enough to know that they had to be in agreement before anything could get done in the Fellowship.*[29]

Dr. Bob may have had a simple message, but his example of kindness and consideration lives on in the lives of AA members worldwide. The flame that became Alcoholics Anonymous was lit in Akron, and Dr. Bob was the steady breeze that caused that flame to burn and spread. I heard Dr. Bob's son say that if it was up to his father AA would have never gotten beyond Akron. I think Smitty was wrong. Dr. Bob was responsible for much of AA's growth and his real contribution to AA still echoes in meetings throughout the world. Each time a member offers encouragement, love, and a pat on the back to another member, Dr. Bob's spirit is manifest.

chapter five

The Princess and the Prince

THE PREVIOUS CHAPTER TOLD about AA's growth in Akron and Dr. Bob's contribution to those early members. I also shared Bill W.'s comment about Dr. Bob's being the "prince of all Twelve Steppers." In a talk at AA's twenty-fifth anniversary convention in Long Beach, California, Bill introduced Sister Ignatia as "Princess Ignatia." Sister Ignatia was the nun who befriended Dr. Bob when she served as a hospital administrator in Akron. She worked alongside Dr. Bob for many years and was known affectionately as the "Little Sister of AA." This chapter provides another perspective on Dr. Bob through his work with Sister Ignatia.

Bill gave credit to many non-alcoholic people throughout the years. He would often say, "AA has many founders." Recognizing and praising non-alcoholics who were instrumental in some phase of AA's development or were helpful in his own spiritual growth was always a priority for Bill. He often mentioned the names Sam Shoemaker, Henrietta Seiberling, T. Henry and Clarace Williams, Dr. Walter Tunks, Dr. William D. Silkworth, Dr. Harry Tiebout, Charles Towns, Father Ed Dowling, John D. Rockefeller, Anne Smith, and, of course, Sister Ignatia.

When talking about sponsorship at the Long Beach conference in 1960, Bill W. said the following.

> In the early days of AA, there were far more customers than there
> were sober AAs to do Twelve Step work. This was especially true
> in the days of Bob and Sister Ignatia. And we ought to remember
> them when we think of sponsorship and the Twelve Steps. And in
> this connection, and as a permanent memorial of what they did,
> we put a plaque on the wall of St. Thomas Hospital in Akron, which
> would commemorate and renew in our memory the Twelve Step
> job that was done there by that dedicated couple.[30]

In late June 1965, a golden anniversary celebration for
Sister Ignatia was held at St. Thomas Hospital. Many of the
early Akron and Cleveland members were present, and some
shared their thoughts of these times and of Sister Ignatia. Bill
W. was the guest speaker and his comments resonated with
deep humility and love. His talk seemed out of character for
him because he didn't offer his usual stories about AA's early
days — affectionately called "bedtime stories" by some. Among
the attendees were many people associated with the Catholic
Church and St. Thomas Hospital, which may explain Bill's
departure from his norm.

Here's what Bill shared on that summer evening in Akron.

> We of AA stand upon the threshold of our fourth decade. In the
> passage of our short years, we know that the time has arrived
> when our society stands wholly on its own, supported by the
> grace of God. This fellowship could never have been born in the
> first place, nor prospered since, without the ministrations of its
> great friends. We are gathered here to pay tribute especially to
> one. And if I may avail myself of this unique hour, which will
> never return to any of us, I would like to make it inclusive and say
> what I believe this society owes the church.
>
> The succession from the Master Himself has brought to us
> light by which we may see and love, by which we may try to

emulate. To me, the keynote of this occasion was so well struck when the Prayer of [St.] Francis opened it; and when Eddie G. said that it was this outpouring of wisdom and love that finally opened his eyes toward a faith that works.

I was one step further removed in my early days with faith. I had none, and virtually no instructions. As a child in a little Vermont town, I looked [at the church] with a certain amount of awe. The church was mysterious. Some said to me that it was even fearsome. I'm happy to say that my parents didn't say this, but it was in the air.

So the long sequence of events that I have so often recounted about myself finally culminated in my being given a sudden illumination, if you like, in which I comprehended a small fraction of that ultimate reality that is God. Truly a gift of grace, for I had no faith as a condition precedent. I just cried in the dark as a child alone, to whatever God there might be and I received a gift of faith — faith of sorts. I still knew nothing of religion; in fact, at such a late time as the book was done [April 1939], I would toy with the childhood idea that Catholicism is a superstition, particularly of the Irish.

10 Over at Dr. Bob's house, the childhood memories of a few sessions at Congregational Sunday school were revived, when there we listened to Anne read from James that "faith without works is dead." . . . I think the beginning of my appreciation was made when I first contacted one of the greats of this wondrous church. He came to me across the centuries through the words of a biography written, I think, by a non-Catholic.

And at length my eyes fell upon this prayer, which says, "This, Bill, is all that you or anyone could possibly aspire to." Just like the newcomer who comes into AA saying of his sponsor, "This guy practices what he preaches" — so did I look upon Francis as I moved out of the kindergarten and into the first-grade experience.

The book was done after this experience, and, as we know, the ideas that went into it stemmed from many sources. But always there was centered in my mind this man of poverty, this man of wisdom, this man of love almost beyond compare, and then came my next experience. By that I mean an experience in which the language of love was so spoken from the heart that it reached me deeply.

After the book came out, I received a letter from a Jesuit in the Sodality at St. Louis. He called himself Ed Dowling, and he sent me a short piece that he had written in the Sodality magazine after looking through our new book, which had been launched as a ship on the great world tide of alcoholism. Ed had looked at the book, and he was saying to the Catholic world, "Folks, this is good; come and get it."

It was some time before I saw this man — one night in the Clubhouse in New York [the 24th Street Clubhouse], Lois being out and this being the only place, by the way, that we could live after being evicted from the house. Because of the book, we went broke, etc., etc. It was empty that night except for I, who was upstairs with an imaginary ulcer attack, feeling awfully sorry for myself. I thought how unappreciative these drunks are of my efforts. As I so meditated, slightly off the St. Francis beam it must be admitted, Old Tom M., an ex-fireman who was the caretaker, clumped up the rickety stairs and he said, "Bill, there's some damn bum from St. Louis wanting to see you."

I said, "My God, Tom, not another one?"

I might background this scene now coming into view by telling you that it was half-past ten at night. The sleet was beating down on the tin roof over my head and it was wild, bitter, and windy outside. I soon heard a step more forwarding than Tom's on the stairs and I still lay on the bed; after all, why should I get up for a bum from St. Louis? Then the figure stood in the door and he wore a battered black hat with an overcoat. Only when he sat down, paying no attention to my lack of courtesy as I lay on the bed, he threw back his collar and I saw that he was a clergyman. He said, "Hello Bill, I'm Father Ed, your Sodality friend in St. Louis. It's been nice to exchange some letters with you."

So of course, I got to be all attention. I began to dimly realize what he had done, so for once I didn't talk; I listened. If you were to hear a recording of what he said and my brief reply, you would say that it was a very superficial visit. But as this man spoke, the room began to fill up with a sense of presence until I could not mistake the fact that here was one of the blessed — one of the many blessed of this church, of which I yet knew nothing.

And this began a communication in the language of the heart with Ed that only ended when he came to my twenty-fifth anniversary. As many of you may know, he had been hideously crippled; he had an unheard of blood pressure and embolisms, and all sorts of things. When people would commiserate with him, Ed would good-naturedly say, "You know, it isn't a bad deal to be this way — people pity you so much." This is how he talked.

He came to my twenty-fifth anniversary and he brought an oxygen mask so he wouldn't suffocate in the plane. The next day, which was a cold day a little reminiscent of that first evening in the Club, we sat in an apartment in the hotel and we chatted about times gone by. Ed said to me, "Bill, I think I should go over to St. Pat's and say a Mass. I presume you have plenty to do?" This was his gentle insinuation that I might go over.

We went out into the vestment room and I saw him don his garb for Mass, and then he said it for me. He then went back to St. Louis and a few weeks later in an AA's home, still talking in this singular language of the heart that was his, he died. Only, of course he didn't know, but we know — all of us — that he dwells in one of our Father's mansions, where many great gentlefolk have gone before us.

Now, I wish to tell you about Sister. I don't suppose I have ever laid it out as plainly as I'm going to. I used to say that she was a female Ed Dowling, but I think that misses the mark by a great deal. She too has her uniqueness, her God-given ways of speaking in this language of the heart. This is not singular to her; I find it all through the church — people who do that. It happens to be because of my special relations and propinquity perhaps with Father Ed and Sister that I would say that these are the channels through which I learned the meaning of the church, so far as I have learned it.

It has now gone down into history what this great partnership [Sister Ignatia and Dr. Bob] has meant in terms of numbers. Some five thousand have passed through here [St. Thomas Hospital, Akron] between 1940 and 1950 in that unforgettable and never to be duplicated partnership of Dr. Bob and Sister. And then we all know about the ward at Charity [St. Vincent Charity Hospital, Cleveland] where she carried on and ministered to ten thousand more.

Numbers have a certain impact, but it is not within anybody's comprehension to know — only God knows this — what the inner meaning of her life has been to those she ministered to and who in turn ministered to still others, in terms of misery ended and in terms of spiritual growth set under way. And yes, if you like, in terms of salvation, only our Lord could know the score. I suppose saying this, as best I can, is the understatement of the year.

I have, for this very special occasion, dispensed with protocol. AA tradition sort of curtly warns us against endorsements and alliances and I have taken my departure from that too, because this is between us folks here and we know what we are talking about. Now downstairs [St. Thomas Hospital, Akron] there are a few words on a plaque that was placed there a good many years ago. I think Dr. Bob was alive at the time, but Anne had gone if my memory serves me right.

That plaque bears this title, "In Gratitude, the friends of Dr. Bob and Anne Smith affectionately dedicate this memorial to the Sisters and to the staff of St. Thomas Hospital at Akron, the birthplace of Alcoholics Anonymous. St. Thomas Hospital became the first religious institution ever to open its doors to our society. May the loving devotion of those who labored in our pioneering time be a bright and wondrous example of God's grace everlastingly set before us all."

And so way back then, we tried to say the things that I have again been trying to say here, and, as a matter of fact, somebody asked who wrote that plaque. I said, confessing very quickly, "Well, I did and I think it's a pretty damn good one."

Now at the time that we put that testament of AA's affection on the wall for this hospital, for this Order, and implied this wondrous partnership between the church and us, I very naturally wanted to slip in Sister Ignatia's name. And you know, she has a way of being firm—she only had to say it once. So it doesn't show it downstairs.

A while back, thinking of the blessings that have rained upon us from this place and from Charity [Hospital] and from this church I concocted a private plot of my own, and remembering that she wouldn't appear on here, I said, "I'm not going to ask her this time. I'll cook up another little tract [plaque] trying to say what we think of her and of this Order. I'll just privately take it out to her and I will say, 'I realize, dear Sister, that this is a presumption, but here it is.'"

So she looked at it and she couldn't say, "Oh, no," because it was complete. The result was that a very small group met down in the dining room and it was presented. I think it was her intention to stow it away in a trunk. I don't know if nuns have lockers under their beds or not.

We were coming down to visit the Motherhouse so I toted the new plaque along. And when the good Mother over there set eyes on it, she looked rather sharply at Sister and said in her most authoritarian manner, "Sister, you are to hang this on the wall in your office!"

Well, this is it. Again, I'm trying to say this for AA members throughout the world because if they were in my place they would all say it, and this testament reads as follows: "In gratitude for Sister Mary Ignatia on the occasion of her Golden Jubilee." Dear Sister, we of AA look upon you as the finest friend and the greatest spirit that we may ever know. We remember your tender ministrations to us in the days when AA was very young. Your partnership with Dr. Bob in that early time created for us a spiritual heritage of incomparable worth. In all the years since, we have watched you at the bedsides of thousands. And so watching, we have perceived ourselves to be the beneficiaries of that wondrous light that God has always sent through you to illumine our darkness. You have tirelessly tended our wounds; you have nourished us with your unique understanding and your matchless love. No greater gift of grace than this shall we ever have. Speaking for all AA members throughout the world, I say, "May God abundantly reward you according to your blessed work, now and forever."[31]

Undoubtedly, Bill loved Sister Ignatia and was very grateful for all of her contributions. It seems that everyone loved and appreciated her. When I was interviewing some of AA's long-time members for the book *1000 Years of Sobriety*, I had the pleasure of including Frank C.'s story. Frank was from Cleveland, and he had the opportunity to go through Rosary Hall, an alcoholic ward at St. Vincent Charity Hospital, while Sister Ignatia was there. This is what he shared with me.

> I went through the program at Rosary Hall with Sister Ignatia. She was a tough one, but she loved the work. When I completed the program, Sister Ignatia gave me a little book that I still read today. It was entitled "Confidence in God" and gives words of encouragement. I've worn out my copy of this wonderful book over the years. Sister Ignatia also handed out Sacred Heart Medallions and told the recipients that if they were going to take a drink, they had to return the medallion first. When I asked, "Where's my medallion," she replied, "You? No, Frank, you won't make it a week." Then she said, "I don't waste them on guys like you." She could tell I wasn't sincere.[32]

Frank went on to tell me that he had stayed sober for only four days after getting out of the Rosary Hall program. Although he was never able to re-enter the program as a patient, he often went there for meetings during his more than fifty years of sobriety. He was very fond of Sister Ignatia and deeply appreciated and respected her.

Bill W. demonstrated his admiration for Sister Ignatia by continually crediting her contributions to AA service through her Twelve Step work. In 1951 in San Francisco, the American Public Health Association presented the Lasker Award to Alcoholics Anonymous "in recognition of its unique and highly successful approach" to an "age-old public health and social problem, alcoholism."[33] On the eve of the presentation, Bill spoke at the San Francisco Opera House. In his speech, he paid tribute to Sister Ignatia.

> **11** Too few know the story of our next great friend in the town of Akron. That friend is one that every AA within a thousand miles can name. She is Sister Ignatia, a frail nun at the Catholic hospital in Akron, St. Thomas — the first religious institution ever to open its door to our society. She had known the doctor in his drinking time; she saw him sober. The city hospital had grown tired of this new-fangled nonsense. The Sister began to slip drunks into beds that other people should have had, all because Smithy wanted her to. And by and by the staff of the hospital became interested and asked Doc Smith to join them, although he wasn't a Catholic.
>
> So Smithy and Sister Ignatia began their classic Twelve Step job. And the example of that dear lady has been something of a quality of inspiration I could never describe to you. We alcoholics talk about how we do our Twelve Step work. That frail one rises at five in the morning and never goes to bed until eleven or twelve and almost never leaves the premises. Nearly all her waking hours are devoted to alcoholics, and before Dr. Bob died she and he had ministered to five thousand cases in that one hospital. Who says AA has only two founders?[34]

Bill's questioning AA having only two founders illustrates his way of shifting the credit from himself onto others in a genuine act of humility as he practiced the spiritual principles. Both Dr. Bob and Sister Ignatia deserved the title of prince and princess, respectively, in regard to carrying the AA message.

In 1960, when Bill W. introduced Sister Ignatia to the guests at AA's twenty-fifth anniversary convention in Long Beach, she endeared herself to the crowd with her charm, her quick wit, and her love for the alcoholics and their families. This had been demonstrated by her selfless work with some of the most desperate cases over the previous twenty years.

Bill's introduction of Sister Ignatia was among the warmest he had ever spoke. Perhaps her relationship with Dr. Bob caused Bill to have an even deeper love and affection toward her. This was how he chose to present her on that warm Southern California afternoon.

> We've got out here one of the dearest friends that this society could ever have. She wouldn't admit it; she's on the frail side. By common sense standards she shouldn't have been here, but she couldn't help it. I'm referring to Sister Ignatia and I wish that every one of you could know her as Dr. Bob and I—and all those to whom she ministered—knew her.
>
> The whole world and this world of ours, this "AA"—individuals, groups, societies, governments, and alike—are always a process of choosing destruction, mediocrity, or greatness in spirit and action. In AA we say that our Twelve Step work—this carrying the message to the other fella or gal—is our move toward greatness in action and spirit, in our modest way.
>
> Practically any active AA has done some Twelve Step jobs—maybe a score, maybe a hundred. But what about a person who has done twelve thousand! And I won't stop with the quantity; the quality, after all, was the thing because this was Dr. Bob's partner. And this lady was certainly—if we call Dr. Bob the "prince of all of the Twelve Steppers"—the "princess." And I introduce you to "Princess Ignatia."[35]

More than ten thousand AAs, family, and friends rose to greet the Sister with a standing ovation, which must have seemed to her to go on far too long. It's unlikely that she had ever received any recognition of this type or would have wanted it. This frail little nun stood up to the microphone and gave many AAs their first glimpse of her. When the crowd settled down, Sister Ignatia opened her brief comments very humbly.

Well, I feel that there is no credit coming to me for this. I feel this
is a privilege that God could pick out such a weak instrument to
take part in such a great movement. As I little thought when Dr.
Bob first talked with me about this that it would turn into such
a wonderful work of God. It's only when we appear before our
judgment seat will we know all that has transpired in the souls
that have come in contact with this movement. Homes have been
rehabilitated and lives have been completely changed. Only those
of us who are at the vantage point, where we are seeing them
coming and going and trying to follow through, have just a little
idea — but in God's way, how tremendous. May God bless every
one of you and give you years of happiness here and eternity of
happiness hereafter. God bless you![36]

At another gathering at the Long Beach convention, Sister
Ignatia captivated her audience for thirty minutes with her recollections of the early days of AA. The chairman of the meeting
introduced her with these kind words.

I looked forward to this opportunity of chairing the meeting
because this would give me an opportunity to meet her. I am very
happy that she has been able to come to the Coast and be with us
here this afternoon, so you may feel and come to know the sweetness of her spirit and the depth of her concern and the effectiveness of her service to suffering alcoholics: Sister Ignatia.[37]

After a few brief opening remarks, Sister Ignatia said the
following.

How little I thought when I entered the convent that I would
spend my days, at least as many of them as I have, in caring
for alcoholics. But God works in mysterious ways and certainly
His divine providence has directed all this. . . . He can use very
weak instruments to carry out His designs, but in our vantage
point, as I know Colonel Towns would say, you see many wonderful results, nothing short of miracles. We are not given to a lot

of imaginary things, but certainly God is extremely kind to the alcoholics.

Author's note: Colonel Towns was also a guest on the program. He was the son of Charles B. Towns, founder of Towns Hospital, where Bill W. had his spiritual experience.

She continued talking about being privileged to do this type of work and then began talking about when she was first sent to Akron. She had been assigned there as "occupational therapy" — "A change of occupation for a while — I was in the field of music and, as you know, that's rather nerve racking." Of course, the crowd of alcoholics enjoyed her sense of humor!

I was sent to St. Thomas [Hospital], which was just opened in 1928, and it was there I met Dr. Bob. We had an open staff the first years because we didn't know the men nor did they know us. Doctor operated at our hospital and at the other hospitals. I didn't know that he had a drinking problem and, in fact, I wouldn't have known it had he not told me so, because he didn't come to the hospital while he was drinking, evidently. Oh, I can recall that sometimes his voice was rather reverberating. I could hear him when he came in the back door. He had a decided New England accent. But I liked him because he was so straightforward. Those of us who have worked around hospitals know some doctors make everything an emergency — a matter of life or death — while others will tell you the exact truth about the case. . . .

One day he looked rather down. We often had little chats, and this morning I said, "What's the trouble this morning?"

He said, "Well, Sister, I might as well tell you. I came in contact with a New York broker and I've had a drinking problem for a long time. And somehow we've got together and have tried to work out something that will help these drunks." He said, "We've been trying it and have tried it out and have had some in the rest homes, and he had some in the other hospitals. Sister, would you consider taking one?"

Well, I hesitated, because sometime before, probably several months, I took a man in. I didn't know much about this drinking. I knew some could drink and handle it well while others couldn't. So they called me down to emergency and I went down and talked with him, and he said, "Sister, if I could just lie down a little while?"

He worked at the city garage and looked like a very respectable person, and saying he's been drinking a little too much and wanted to get straightened out, which I felt was a good thing. The only bed we had at the time was one in a four-bed room. This was when we knew nothing about special treatment and I assigned him to the man on medical service, registered him, and put him to bed saying, "You won't cause any trouble." Oh no, he'd be an angel.

I had forgotten about him, but when I came over early the next morning, the night supervisor was standing at the door waiting for me. She said, "The next time you take a DT in this place, please stay up all night and run after him like we have." I decided then that that's enough and I often felt sorry to see them turned away, but I wasn't the last word in the hospital.

So when Doctor proposed my taking a real one, you can imagine my misgivings. I thought, "Oh dear me." I told him about this last experience and said, "Doctor, not only will I be put out, but the patients, and everyone else. I don't think they want alcoholics."

He said, "Sister, this patient won't give you a bit of trouble because I will medicate him, and I will assure you." I had much confidence in him [Dr. Bob] because he never said anything that wasn't so.

Very fearfully I said, "Yes, Doctor, I shall take him then, and put him in a two-bed room." I thought I was doing pretty well because we were so crowded in those days and the beds were rather a premium. So I took him to the two-bed room and Doctor went up and medicated him and everything. And I felt I wouldn't hear much until the next morning, even if there was any trouble.

Doctor then came to the admitting office and said, "Sister, would you mind putting my patient in a private room?" I thought

I'd done pretty good to put him in a two-bed room. He explained that there would be some men coming to visit him and they would like to talk to him privately.

I said, "I'll do what I can." After he left I went up to look the situation over and right across the hall was the flower room where we used to prepare the patients' flowers. I thought, "I believe they can fix the flowers somewhere else for today and I can push the bed in there." So I did!

Sister Ignatia continued, describing how St. Thomas Hospital began to welcome the alcoholic patients, starting first with the flower room, and then a two-bed room (both beds with alcoholic patients), and then a four-bed room, and so on. The progress seemed slow but nevertheless steady as this institution opened its doors to AA. She went on to share the following experience.

A committee from Alcoholics Anonymous talked with Sister Superior. She was one who had a lot of experience in the old days at Charity and she knew what we were doing. She said to these men that when they had them [alcoholics] at Charity they would be running the halls and doing a lot of trouble. But since Dr. Bob was treating them we didn't know that they were in the house. So, she said that there was no problem as far as she could see — so just go right along.

Sister Ignatia related that the AAs got so much attention and so many visitors that other patients complained that the alcoholics were being given special privileges. Sister then shared how Dr. Bob started the first alcoholic ward.

We had a small accident ward, which was sort of off from the rest of the hospital, and there we put in a "coffee bar." Dr. Bob set up the program. The first opportunity he had, he brought Bill over and, of course, I couldn't imagine who this wonderful Bill was. But I soon learned that God had chosen two great men. What one didn't have, the other supplemented and together they were perfect. I often say to our boys [the men on the ward at Cleveland Rosary Hall] that had God picked out two great religious leaders no one would have come near them. Because the alcoholic doesn't want anything with religion or God, nor do we try to preach religion to them.

They're [the alcoholic patients] not in very long until they're asking or telling you what experience they've had and what they would like to do. They know they haven't been living right. I feel, as many of our nurses have said, that the best sedative is "peace of mind." Once they can be relieved of their anxieties and worries and treated properly, they should be no trouble.

When they first came in—no televisions, no radios, and no newspapers—only literature pertaining to AA or something that would build their morals and things of that kind. They had all the reading they could take care of and then their visitors.

AA literature was very limited in the early years. The only book available was the Big Book (*Alcoholics Anonymous,* first published in 1939). By 1943, the Alcoholic Foundation's publishing company, known as Works Publishing, had produced several pamphlets.

Some of the groups began to come up with pamphlets of their own and Akron spearheaded those efforts. Nevertheless, it seems apparent that the early program in the ward at St. Thomas Hospital was Alcoholics Anonymous—one member sharing his story, experience, strength, and hope with the next. Sister Ignatia then had this to say about Dr. Bob.

> During Doctor's time I think we treated between four and five
> 12 thousand, and he treated them. He came in every day, unless
> he was out of town or something, without any charge. He said,
> "That's my contribution to AA." Of course in those days [the
> alcoholics] didn't have too much to start with. You couldn't mention money or how much it would cost. If we could just get them
> sober, it would mean a great deal. But that was taken care of

later on, thank God. It worked out very well and there were no problems; whether they had it or not, we took them in. God certainly provides. The man who "gets" this program is everlastingly grateful.

It was hard to understand, but sometimes [Dr. Bob] would make rounds and come down and say, "Sister, let that man go home. He doesn't want this program."

"Oh, but Doctor, he has a big family, and this, that, and the other."

"He doesn't want the program, Sister — he isn't ready!" He was always right.

Many times they would be frightened, having had a heart attack or a bad heart or something, and I hated to bother the doctor too much, so often I'd call Anne.

I think members of Alcoholics Anonymous should say a prayer for her because she was the backbone of this, in her calm, quiet way. She was an angel. I would call her and tell her, "I'm worried about this fellow."

She knew most of them either from reputation or Doctor telling about them. And she would get the doctor if it was anything serious, but otherwise she would say, "Don't worry about this."

We would take them but once; that was Doctor's plan too. I thought, "Oh my, that's kind of strict, isn't it? But I see the wisdom of it. Because if there is a merry-go-round, when that temptation comes, they'll think, "Well, I can get back in there for five or six days. Sister's all right, she'll take me back." And I'd only be encouraging them in drinking. They know this is only a one-time trip.[38]

As she continued her talk in Long Beach, Sister Ignatia discussed the importance of sponsorship, as she often did throughout her career of working with alcoholics. All of the people admitted to the program at St. Thomas Hospital in Akron, as well as Rosary Hall in Cleveland, had to be sponsored by an AA member in good standing.

"Dr. Bob's Story" in the Big Book, and other accounts from early AA members he sponsored, show that he stressed the seriousness of the illness. He also made clear how the practice of talking to other alcoholics must be taken seriously. Perhaps that is why "sponsorship" became such a vital and important part of AA.

chapter six

"Let's Not Louse It All Up"

PREVIOUS CHAPTERS DISCUSSED Dr. Bob's contributions to AA's growth, his emphasis on the importance of sponsorship, and his service as a medical professional alongside Sister Ignatia. In this chapter, I want to call attention to perhaps his greatest contribution — reminding us to "Keep it simple." I also want to share a tribute from his son, Bob Jr. (Smitty), and, finally, let Dr. Bob tell his own story.

In an article titled "A Tribute to Dr. Bob" in the January 1951 issue of the *Grapevine*, Bill W. praised him and reminisced about Dr. Bob's many contributions to AA and to himself. It has been mentioned in AA literature that Bill W. was Dr. Bob's sponsor. However, the wise counsel and example Dr. Bob gave to Bill also resembles the relationship AA members describe having with their sponsor. In other words, in many ways Dr. Bob was Bill's sponsor, too. Dr. Bob was a stable and respected force in Bill's life, and he influenced Bill extensively on important AA decisions, as Bill noted in the *Grapevine* tribute.

How we were spared from professionalism, wealth, and extensive property management; how we finally came up with the book Alcoholics Anonymous *is a story by itself. But in this critical period it was Dr. Bob's prudent counsel which so often restrained us from rash ventures that might have retarded us for years, perhaps ruined us for good. Nor can we ever forget the devotion of Dr. Bob and Jim S. (who passed away last summer) as they gathered stories for the AA Book, three-fifths of them coming from Akron alone. Dr. Bob's special fortitude and wisdom were prime factors in that time so much characterized by doubt, and finally by grave decision.*

How much we may rejoice that Anne and Dr. Bob both lived to see the lamp lit at Akron carried into every corner of the earth; that they doubtless realized millions might someday pass under the ever-widening arch whose keystone they so gallantly helped carve. Yet, being so humble as they were, I'm sure they never quite guessed what a heritage they left us, nor how beautifully their appointed task had been completed. All they needed to do was finished. It was even reserved for Dr. Bob to see AA come of age as, for the last time, he spoke to 7000 of us at Cleveland, July, 1950.

AA's First International Convention in 1950 marked several of AA's most significant historical moments. For example, this is when the AA Traditions were officially adopted. The theme of the convention was "We've Come of Age." Dr. Bob, who had been suffering from cancer and spent most of his time in bed, was able to make a brief appearance and deliver what turned out to be his farewell address.

My good friends in AA and of AA, I feel I would be very remiss if I didn't take this opportunity to welcome you here to Cleveland. Not only to this meeting, but those that have already transpired. I hope very much that they have the presence of so many people and the words that you've heard will prove an inspiration to you — not only to you, but may you be able to impart that inspiration to the boys and girls back home who are not fortunate enough to be able to come. In other words, we hope that your visit here has been both enjoyable and profitable.

I get a big thrill at looking out over a vast sea of faces like this with a feeling that possibly some small thing that I did a number of years ago played a small part in making this meeting possible. I also get quite a thrill when I think that we all had the same problem, we all did the same things, we all get the same results in proportion to our zeal and enthusiasm and stick-to-itiveness.

13 If you'll pardon the injection of a personal note at this time, let me say that I've been in bed five of the last seven months and my strength hasn't returned as I like so I'll out of necessity be very brief. But there are two or three things that flashed into my mind on which it would be fitting to lay a little emphasis. One is the simplicity of our program. Let's not louse it all up with Freudian complexes and things that are interesting to the scientific mind but have very little to do with our actual AA work.

Our Twelve Steps, when simmered down to the last, resolve themselves into the words "love" and "service." We understand what love is and we understand what service is. So let's bear those two things in mind.

Let us also remember to guard that erring member, the tongue, and if we must use it, let's use it with kindness and consideration and tolerance. And one more thing, none of us would be here today if somebody hadn't taken time to explain things to us, to give us a little pat on the back, to take us to a meeting or two, to have done numerous little, kind, and thoughtful acts on our behalf. So let us never get the degree of smug complacency so that we're not willing to extend or attempt to that help that has been so beneficial to us, to our less fortunate brothers. Thank you very much.[39]

In this speech, which lasted less than four minutes, Dr. Bob encapsulated perhaps the most important elements of AA. He saw that big meetings such as the one being held in Cleveland were inspirational, and he encouraged those present to carry that inspiration to alcoholics unable to attend.

Author's note: *The sense of fellowship and the power present at this large gathering is recreated every five years when AA members gather for their international convention. The 2010 convention was held in San Antonio,*

Texas, where more than fifty thousand anonymous friends gathered to celebrate AA's seventy-fifth anniversary. At the big meeting in the Alamo dome on Saturday night, the audience heard the words of Dr. Bob played over the PA system.

Next, Dr. Bob suggests that all AAs are the same. The idea of recognizing the similarities among members, and not the differences, has been one of AA's strong links. Dr. Bob says "we all did the same things" and "we all had the same problem." He emphasizes that AA members all receive the same results in proportion to their zeal, enthusiasm, and stick-to-itiveness.

Dr. Bob selected several other simple, yet profoundly important, characteristics or principles that members ought to consider. The first he prefaces under the heading of "simplicity" and then warns, "Let's not louse it all up with Freudian complexes and things that are interesting to the scientific mind but have very little to do with our actual AA work."

Author's note: *Sigmund Freud's views on alcoholism would probably amaze modern audiences. For instance, in a letter to Wilhelm Fliess on December 22, 1897, Freud refers to masturbation as the "primary addiction." His statement reads, "The insight has dawned on me that masturbation is the one major habit, the 'primary addiction,' and it is only as a substitute and replacement for it that the other addictions — to alcohol, morphine, tobacco, and the like — come into existence."* [40]

But to think that he was simply saying "Keep it simple" would oversimplify his message. Consider his comment, "Our Twelve Steps, when simmered down to the last, resolve themselves into the words 'love' and 'service.'" [41] Dr. Bob stays with a simple approach, but how many AAs would really consider simmering down the Twelve Steps to just two things? His insight into the importance of "love" and "service" is remarkable. These words are not found in the Twelve Steps. Yet Dr. Bob concludes that when the Steps are condensed, this would be the result.

(Certainly, and deservingly, Dr. Bob has been recognized and credited as a very spiritual man, but it would be a mistake to ignore his scientific education and training. His uncanny ability to dissect incredibly challenging propositions and communicate them in simple terms should not be discounted.)

He continues by issuing yet another warning, this in regard to the use of the erring member "the tongue." We are to use it with kindness, consideration, and tolerance. He then reminds his audience to offer a pat on the back to the new guy. They wouldn't be there if someone hadn't offered those services to them: "to take us to a meeting or two, to have done numerous little, kind, and thoughtful acts on our behalf."

His closing comments were perhaps among the most powerful words he ever shared with AA: "So let us never get the degree of smug complacency so that we're not willing to extend or attempt to that help that has been so beneficial to us, to our less fortunate brothers."

It has been said that if you really want to know about someone's character and the way a person really lives, ask his or her children. Dr. Bob and Anne S. had two children, Bob Jr. (Smitty) and Sue, their adopted daughter. Although both Bob Jr. and Sue knew Bill W. and were around when AA was first being developed, they were teenagers, busy with school and their social lives, and thus not closely involved. Still, it was Smitty who drove his mother and father to the Seiberling estate for their first meeting with Bill W.

Neither Bob Jr. nor Sue became alcoholics, but they did receive invitations to speak at AA conferences and "roundups." Smitty enjoyed sharing memories of his parents and the challenges they faced both with alcoholism and with AA, once it began.

Because of a mutual friend, I was able to visit with Bob Jr. a few times during the late 1980s while I was living in Texas. I enjoyed hearing firsthand experiences about Dr. Bob and Anne, and listening to Smitty speak was a pleasure. I attended an open meeting in Kerrville, Texas, in 1986 where Smitty was one of the featured speakers. He shared some wonderful insights into his father's personality.

> I'll take a little time to describe my father, Dr. Bob, to you. Dr. Bob was a wonderful father to me. He was a tall, thin Vermonter with icy blue eyes. He graduated from Dartmouth College, one of the Ivy League colleges in the East. He worked in industry for a while and came back and prevailed on his father, who was a probate judge there in St. Johnsbury, to put him through medical school. He managed to get through medical school in Chicago, although his drinking was already taking a terrible toll and he just barely got out of there.
>
> He managed to obtain a coveted internship in Akron, Ohio. They had some advanced equipment there at the time so he was allowed to come there. He married my mother after a whirlwind courtship of only seventeen years. Dr. Bob didn't do anything in a hurry!
>
> Bill W. was also a tall, thin Vermonter and they were raised within a hundred miles of each other, although they never had met. But they were just the opposite. Bill was garrulous; he loved to meet people, he loved to talk, he was a visionary, he could see way up the road. My father was a steadier type. He didn't have a whole lot to say, but these two guys fit together perfectly. You know, if any two of us were exactly alike — one of us is unnecessary.
>
> Dr. Bob was a general practitioner there in Akron for several years. And then he went on and studied under the Mayo brothers in Rochester, Minnesota, at the Mayo Clinic and became a surgeon. He did nothing but surgery for the balance of his professional life. Well, they wore those short surgical gowns when they operated, and Dr. Bob had a dragon tattooed on his left arm that started at his shoulder and went all the way down to his wrist. This was the source of a lot of embarrassment to him. I said, "My gosh, Dad, how did you ever get that?"
>
> He said, "Boy, that was a dandy!"
>
> Dr. Bob had a beautiful sense of humor and when I brought my bride home for the folks to look over (we were going to be

married) she was tall and thin. He got me aside and said, "She's built for speed and light housekeeping."

I've got to tell you what his sex and hygiene lecture was as a teenager. He took me upstairs into the bathroom and closed the door and sat down and said, "Flies spread disease — keep yours buttoned." [42]

Smitty deeply loved his father and mother, and it became obvious that he loved both AA and Al-Anon. He spent a good deal of time talking with groups about his parents and AA's early days.

Since Dr. Bob was busy with his medical practice and had limited time to travel, very little firsthand information on him is available. The AA World Services publication *Dr. Bob and the Good Oldtimers: A Biography, with Recollections of Early A.A. in the Midwest* makes a great read, but information in the book was gathered from the recollections of early AAs, their families, and friends and is, therefore, difficult to authenticate.

Probably the best look into Dr. Bob's personality and his views on AA come from his story in the Big Book and from a talk given in Detroit in 1948. That speech, which has been labeled "Dr. Bob's last major address," vividly demonstrates his views and his memories of those early days in Akron.

Although a good many of you have heard or have read articles written about the inception of AA, there are probably some who haven't. And from that brief story there are some things to be learned. So even at the risk of repetition, I would like to relate just exactly what did happen in those very early days.

And I feel there is a lesson to be learned and one we must never forget if we wish to maintain that paid-up insurance policy against our drinking. You recall the story about Bill having had some spiritual experience, having been sold on the idea of attempting to be helpful to others. You undoubtedly recall a fact that he had been working quite hard at it for around five months or so, almost incessantly, and still had not created, if you please, a single convert. Not one. As we express it, no one had "jelled." But he had worked tirelessly with no thought of saving his own strength or time or anything. But nothing seemed to register. . . .

Then in October [1935] we had three dumped in our lap, almost simultaneously. But the point I wanted to bring out was the fact that, in my mind, the spirit of service is of prime importance, although it has to be backed up with some knowledge of the subject. I know I used to go to the hospital and I'd stand there and talk; I talked many a time to a chap in a bed for four or five or six hours. I don't know how he ever stood me for five or six hours, but he did. We'd probably hidden his clothes or something.

But anyway, it came to my mind that I probably didn't know too much about what I was talking about. Therefore, we being stewards of what we have, and that includes our time, I was not giving a good account of my stewardship of time. If it took me six hours to say something to this man that I could have said in an hour, we'll say, if I'd known what I was talking about, I certainly was not a very efficient individual.

And incidentally, I'm somewhat allergic to work anyway. So, I felt that I should continue my familiarity not only with the Good Book but read a good deal of good standard literature and possibly something of scientific interest along with it. So I did cultivate this habit of reading and I think I'm not exaggerating when I say I've probably averaged to read an hour a day for the last fifteen years. Now, I don't say that to try to sell you on the idea that you've got to cultivate that habit of reading an hour a day. Because there are plenty of people and fine AAs that don't read very much.

You see back in those days we were groping in the dark entirely. We did not know much about it. We knew practically nothing about alcoholism. I, a physician, knew nothing about it to speak of. I'd read about it. But there wasn't anything worth reading in any of the textbooks. And usually the information about it consisted of some weird treatment for DTs if you'd gone that far and, if you hadn't, why you prescribed a few bromides and gave the fellow a good lecture. None of which amounted to very much.

And in early AA days we became quite convinced that the
spiritual program was fine but that we could help the Lord out a
little with some supplementary diet. So in the early days Bill W.,
having frequent stomach trouble, had stumbled across the fact
he got along much better on sauerkraut and cold tomatoes. And
so we thought that inasmuch as Bill had to have that experience,
that probably everyone else would have to share the same. But,
of course, we discovered later most any dietary restriction had
very little to do with acquisition and maintenance of permanent
sobriety.

Our own stories didn't amount to anything to speak of when
we started in on Bill [AA number three]. We had no Twelve Steps,
we had no Traditions, we had nothing of that kind. But we were
convinced that the answer to our problem was in the Good Book.
And it became somewhat evident, we thought, to some of us older
ones, that it was contained — the part that we found absolutely
essential to a rather limited section of the Good Book; in other
words, the Sermon on the Mount, the thirteenth chapter of [First]
Corinthians, and the book of James. I think we got those ideas
pretty firmly implanted in our minds fairly early.

Our membership got to five, and seven, and ten, and still
small. Why, we used to have daily meetings in somebody's house.
It was probably providentially arranged that all this happened at
a time when everybody was broke, and awfully broke too. It was
probably much easier for us to be successful when broke than
it would have been to have been successful if we'd had a good
checking account apiece.

But I know that we were, every one of us, just so painfully
broke. Well, it wasn't a pleasant thought. But nothing could be
done about it, and everybody else was broke too, and so we didn't
take it too much to heart. But I do think that that was providentially arranged.

But anyway, we kept on having these meetings and having
these discussions and attending the meetings of these good people
[the Oxford Group] with whom we had been associated, and did
continue to have meetings with them until (in Akron I'm talking

about, of course) about '40 or maybe early in '41 — might have been January of '41. I don't recall the exact dates.

When we outgrew the residence of this good friend [T. Henry Williams] who'd allowed us to bang up the plaster and the door jambs, carting chairs up and down — they had a very beautiful home — we stepped out and in a short time acquired the rental of the auditorium in the King School and we — I'm talking about the group I attend personally — have been there ever since. We attempt to have a good meeting, and I think we usually are successful.

But it wasn't until '39 that the teachings and efforts and studies that had been going on were crystallized in the form of the Twelve Steps. I didn't write the Twelve Steps. I had nothing to do with the writing of them. I think probably I had something to do with them indirectly, because after this June 10th episode Bill came to live at our house and stayed for about three months. And there was hardly a night in that three months that we didn't sit up till two or three o'clock discussing these things. And it would be hard for me to conceive that something wasn't said during those nightly discussions around our kitchen table that influenced the actual writing of the Twelve Steps.

They are much more handy to have in that form, of course; we had the ideas pretty much, basically, but not in terse and tangible form. We got them as a result of our study and effort of the Good Book. We must have had them because we have learned from experience that they were very important in main-taining sobriety and we were maintaining sobriety; therefore, we had them but not in exactly the written form as you know them now.

But that is the way that things started off in Akron and as we grew we began to get offshoots. The first one was in Cleveland. I don't remember the next one. But anyway, they were started in Akron not too long after that and have been continuing ever since. It is a great source of satisfaction to me to feel that I may have played some part in kicking in my two-bits-worth towards getting this thing started. I like to think that I have done that; maybe I'm taking too much for granted—I don't know. But I feel that I was simply used as God's agent. I feel that I'm no different from any of you fellows or girls except that I was a little more fortunate—that I got this message thirteen and a half years ago and some of you had to wait till a little later.

In fact, I got a little peeved at our Heavenly Father because I thought He was a little slow on the trigger because I thought I would have been ready to receive it quite a while before He got around to presenting it. And that used to irritate me no end; but after all, maybe He knows better than I.

But I felt sure that I would have been glad to have anything presented that would have been workable and produced the sobriety which I thought, at least, that I wanted so badly. I used to even doubt that at times. I would go to my good friend Henry and say, "Henry, do you think that I want to stop drinking liquor?"

And Henry, being a very charitable soul, said, "Yes, Bob, I'm sure you want to stop."

And I would say, "Well, I can't conceive of any living human who really wanted to do something as badly as I think I want to do it, who could be so total a failure. Henry, I think I'm just one of these want-to, want-to guys.

He said, "No, Bob, I think you want to. We just haven't found the way to work it yet." But anyway that was the way I felt about it.

14   And the fact that my sobriety has been maintained continuously for thirteen and a half years doesn't allow me to think that I'm necessarily any farther away from my next drink than any of you people here. I'm still very human. And I still think a double scotch would taste awful good. *[laughter]* And if it didn't produce disastrous results, I might do it. I don't know. I really love scotch. But I have no reason to think it would taste any differently. I have no legitimate reason to believe that the results would be any different. They were always the same; they were always the same in that I always wound up back of the dear old eight-ball some way. And I have no precedent or anything to make it feel legitimate for me to believe that the results today would be any different than

they were fourteen and twenty and twenty-five and thirty years ago when l did the same thing.

l just don't want to pay that bill because that's a big bill. It always was, and l think it would be even larger today, because with what has gone on in the last thirteen years, and naturally being a bit out of practice, l don't believe I'd really last very long and I'm having an awful nice time and l just don't want to bump myself off even with the pleasures of the alcohol route. Well, I'm not gonna do it. And I'm never gonna do it, as long as l do the things that I'm supposed to do. And l know what those things are. So if l should ever get tight, l certainly never would have anyone to blame for it. It would be done perhaps not with malice of fore-thought, but it certainly would be done as a result at least of extreme carelessness and indifference.

l said l was quite human. And l get to thinking every once and a while, "Well, here's this Smith guy—a smart individual. He's got this liquor situation right by the tail—proved it, demonstrated it, hasn't had a drink for thirteen years. Probably could knock off a couple, and no one would be the wiser."

No, l tell you, I'm not trying to be funny at all, because those thoughts actually enter my mind. And l know just the minute they do just exactly what has happened. You see there in Akron, we have the extreme good fortune, as a great many of you people know, of having a very nice hospital setup at St. Thomas Hospital, with a ward that theoretically accommodates seven but it's stretched a little bit and she [Sister Ignatia] usually has about two or three parked around somewhere. And l, almost invariably, find that l hadn't been paying quite so much attention to the boys in the ward as l should—thus ensures that idea that l probably could polish off a couple.

l think, "Uh-uh, about the boys in the ward. You've been giving them the semi-brush off here for a few days. You better get back on the job, big boy, before you get into trouble." And l pedal right back and be much more attentive than l had been in the days preceding the time that l got this funny idea. But l get it, and l get it every once in a while and I'll probably continue to get it as long as, or whenever, I get careless about that one thing.

You know, back in those early days about which I spoke, before we had the Twelve Steps, we did have some other things besides the actual biblical verses. I was getting to thinking more of Smith than I was of the ward. Otherwise, I wouldn't have neglected them. And I wasn't being especially loving, when these fellas had come there, indicating their desire for help.

And I was just a little too busy to give them any or at least very much of my time. Don't want to be bothered with the burden, ten cents to get rid of them, why that's easy. You could even stand two bits. But not because you love the fella [drunken "bum," perhaps], but just to be relieved of the nuisance of his hanging on your coat sleeve or what have you. No unselfishness. No love indicated in the transaction at all. But I think that the thing that really counts is really giving a service of yourself and almost invariably requires some effort and time of your own.

It isn't a matter of putting a little acquired quiet money in the dish. That helps, and possibly that's indicated too. But that isn't giving much, that is, for the average individual, in days like this when most people get along at least fairly well. That type of giving, I don't believe, would ever keep anyone sober or anywhere near it. But giving of his own effort, and strength, and time is an entirely different matter. I think that is what Bill learned in New York that I didn't get in Akron.

The matter of those "Four Absolutes," we call them — the only yardsticks we had in the early days. I think they still hold good and I still think that they can be extremely helpful. I've found, at times, that questions arise and I want to do the right thing, but the answers are not obvious — you don't know what the right thing is. But almost always, if you check into it carefully by the yardsticks of "absolute honesty, purity, unselfishness, and love," and whatever your decision is checks out pretty well with those four, your answer can't be very far out of the way.

If, however, you do that, as I have done at times, and still are not too satisfied with the answer, I usually consult some friend whose judgment, perhaps, I think, in this particular case would be very much better than mine. But usually you can do it yourself without bothering your friends about your own personal decisions.

In overcoming the First Step, we can't quite get honest enough to admit John Barleycorn really has the best of us. The matter of "absolute purity" is somewhat like this: it's purity of ideas and purity of motive and what-have-you. And unselfishness includes those things that I've just been talking about, not the dime or the two bits to the bum, but actually giving of yourself. And as you well know, the "absolute love" is probably a big word incorporating all three, with a little bit more along with it. I think that that is a very difficult thing to have — absolute love. I don't think any of us will ever get it. But that doesn't mean that we can't try to get it. It was extremely difficult for me and I feel that I never have been very successful at it.

It's very difficult for me to love my fellow man. I didn't dislike him, but I didn't love him unless there was some special reason; I was just indifferent toward him. I wouldn't do him any harm. I would be willing to give a little lift if it didn't require too much effort. I never would injure him at all, but to love him? I just couldn't do it for a long time. And I think that I overcame it, to some extent, when I was forced to do it. Because I was either going to love this bird and attempt to be helpful to him, or I would probably get drunk again.

You could say, "Well, that's just a manifestation of selfishness," which is quite correct. I was selfish to the extent of not wanting Smith hurt. So to keep from getting Smith hurt, I would attempt to go through the motions of being helpful to this other fellow. You can debate it any way you want to, but the fact remains that for the average fellow, absolute love is a thing he will never acquire. I suspect there are a few people who do. I think maybe I know some who come pretty close to it. But I think I could count them on the fingers of one hand. I don't say that in a discouraging manner — I have some wonderful friends — but I'm talking about it in its finer aspects, particularly as it applies to AAs.

I don't think we do anything "well" very much in this world unless we practice it. And I don't believe we do AA work too well unless we practice it. These fellows that go in, break world records in athletic events, or people who win titles in the boxing arena, are people who practice it. They've been practicing it for years, even though they may necessarily be endowed with a lot of physical ability and skill; they still have to practice it. And we have to practice to do a good job in AA.

And there are a number of things that we should practice. We should practice, as I say, acquiring the "spirit of service." We should attempt to acquire some faith, which isn't always easily done, especially for the person who has always been very materialistically minded. If you have a million bucks and your neighbor has nine hundred grand, you're a much better man than your neighbor to the extent of one hundred thousand dollars. And so forth and so on, *ad nauseam*. But I think that it can be acquired. I think that it can be acquired slowly. I think that it is something that has to be cultivated, also. That was not easy for me. I just assume it's difficult for others.

Another thing that is difficult for me, and I probably don't do too well yet, is the matter of tolerance. We're all inclined to have closed minds. And they're pretty tightly closed, too. And that's one reason some people find spiritual teachings difficult. They don't want to find out too much about it, for very personal reasons.

One reason is their fear of being considered effeminate, just for illustration. But anyway, the matter of tolerance towards the other individual's ideas — it's quite important that we do acquire it. I think that I have acquired it; I have much more of it than I did have, although it's not enough to hurt me any yet. Cause if somebody crossed me, why I was apt to make at least a rather caustic remark about it, which I've done many times, much to my regret. And later on, I find the man knew much more about it than I, and I'd been infinitely better off if I'd kept my big mouth shut.

Another thing with which most of us are not overly blessed is the feeling of humility. I don't mean the humility in the sense of Dickens' Uriah Heep [a character in *David Copperfield,* known for his insincerity] at all. I don't mean the doormat variety. I don't think we're necessarily called on to be shoved around and stepped on by anyone; and we have a right to stand up for our rights. I'm talking about the attitude of each and every one of us toward our Heavenly Father.

Christ said, "Of myself I am nothing; my strength cometh from my Father in Heaven." And if He had to say that, how about you and me? But did you say it? Did I say it? No, that's exactly what we didn't say. We were inclined to say, "Well, look us over boys, pretty good, huh?" — that type of attitude. But there was no humility, no sense of having received anything through the grace of our Heavenly Father.

So, if I accomplish something, either in AA activity or socially or in my profession, why, I don't believe I have any right to get cocky about it. It's only through God's grace I did it. I can feel very thankful that I was privileged to do it, to have the recognition which I have received for some activity. But basically, it was only through His kind act. My strength does come from Him, and these things come as a result of His kindness. Who am I to get cocky about it? I should have a very, very humble attitude towards the source of my strength.

And I should also never cease to be grateful for whatever blessings come my way. And I have been blessed, and in very large measure. It doesn't make much difference whether a person is drinking or whether they're sober as far as their ultimate aim is concerned. Whether they're drinking liquor or whether they're not, they're still after the same thing, and that's happiness and peace of mind. I harp about that a great deal because that's what we're all after and all the time. We want those two things; we want happiness and we want peace of mind.

The trouble with us fellows was that we thought we could demand that the world give us happiness in just a particular way in which we wanted to get it, which happened to be by the alcohol route. And we weren't overly successful.

Dr. Bob and Bill W. Speak

But when we take time to find out, and familiarize ourselves with, and put into practice some of the spiritual laws which are necessary to follow to acquire those things, then we find that we get them. And I think I've had them in very large measure: those two things, happiness and peace of mind. And I feel most extremely fortunate and I feel very grateful and thankful that our Heavenly Father has seen fit that I enjoy them.

They're there; anybody can get them who wishes to. But there do seem to be some rules of the game that we have to follow. But they're here and open and free to everyone who wishes to take advantage of them. And by taking advantage of them means the familiarization with them and putting them into practice, and incorporating them into our own thinking and actions. And we're bound and determined to get certain results if we do.

As I said, it is a very great source of pleasure and gratitude to me to feel that maybe I kicked in my two bits toward starting this. But as I said also, I feel that I was simply used as God's agent. The question might arise, "Well, we know what AA's done in the last thirteen years, but how about it from here on? Where do we go from here?" Our membership is now conservatively estimated, at present, around seventy thousand. Where will it be in the increase from here on?

Well, that'll depend on every member of AA. It is possible for us to do so, or not, as we elect. If we fight, shy of what the politicos call "tangling alliances," if we avoid getting messed up with controversial issues such as religious and political issues, the wet and dry problem, and so forth, if we know unity through our central office, if we remember the simplicity of our program, if we continue to remember that our job is to get sober and to stay sober and to help our less fortunate brother in doing the same thing, I doubt very much that we should have very much trouble. And we will continue to grow and thrive and prosper. And I hope we all bear those little things in mind. Maybe there will be some additions to the list, but that roughly tells it fairly well. I hope none of us will ever forget what I just said about helping our less fortunate brother.[43]

chapter seven

AA's Beginnings in New York

YOU'VE NOW READ QUITE A BIT about the early days in Akron and how AA grew from there. During the same period of time, Bill W. was busy in New York helping AA get off the ground.

As AA grew, Bill W. had to decline many opportunities to speak at AA groups. There were just too many groups and being selective as to which offers to accept and which to reject was too much of a task. So as a general rule he declined the group invitations. I was able to find two talks that Bill gave in New York at the Manhattan Group. Both of these talks were given at Christmas time, one in 1953 and the other in 1955.

The 1955 talk gives a lot of information about AA's early days in New York. Bill reminisced with some of the funny stories and the struggles of those days.

> Now let's start on our story. First of all, there was the kitchen table, which stood in a brownstone house which still bears the number 182 Clinton Street, Brooklyn. There, Lois saw me go into the depths. From there I went to Towns Hospital for the last time. It was there, over the kitchen table, Ebby, one alcoholic talking to another, brought me these simple principles now enshrined in our Twelve Steps.

In those days, there were but six steps: We admitted we couldn't run our lives. We got honest with ourselves. We made a self-survey. We made restitution to the people we had harmed. We tried to carry this story one to the next; and we asked God to help us to do those things. That was the essence of the message over the kitchen table. In those days, we were associated with the Oxford Group. One of its founders was Sam Shoemaker, and this group [the Manhattan Group] has just left Calvary House to come over to these larger quarters, I understand.

But our debt to those people is simply immense. We might have found these principles elsewhere, but they did give them to us, and I want to again record our undying gratitude. We also learned from them, so far as alcoholics are concerned, what not to do — something equally important. A great Jesuit friend of ours, Ed Dowling, once said to me, "Bill, it isn't what you people put into AA that makes it so good; it's what you left out."

We got both sets of notions from our Oxford Group friends, and it was through them that Ebby had sobered up and became my sponsor, the carrier of this message to me. We began to go to Oxford Group meetings right over in Calvary House, where you've just been gathering, and it was there, fresh out of Towns Hospital, that I made my first pitch, telling about my strange experience, which did not impress the alcoholic who was listening. But something else did impress him. When I began to talk about the nature of this sickness, this malady, he pricked up his ears. He was a professor of chemistry, an agnostic, and he came up and talked afterward.

Soon, he was invited over to Clinton Street, our very first customer. We worked very hard with Freddy for three years, but alas, he remained drunk for eleven years afterward.

Other people came up to us out of those Oxford Group audiences. We began to go down to Calvary Mission, an adjunct of the church in those days, and there we found a bountiful supply of real tough nuts to crack. Soon we began to invite them to Clinton Street, and at this point the Groupers felt that we were overdoing the drunk business. It seemed they had the idea of saving the world; besides, they'd had a bad time with us.

Sam [Shoemaker] and his associates — he now laughingly tells me — were very much put out that they had gathered a big batch of drunks in Calvary House, hoping for a miracle. They'd put them upstairs in those nice apartments and had completely surrounded them with sweetness and light. But they [the drunks] soon imported a flock of bottles, and one of them pitched a shoe out the apartment window right through one of those stained glass affairs of the church. So the drunks weren't exactly popular when the Wilsons showed up.

At any rate, we began to be with alcoholics all the time, but nothing happened for six months. Like the Groupers, we brought them to the house, we nursed them. In fact, over in Clinton Street, we developed in the next two or three years something like a boiler factory, a sort of clinic, a hospital, and a free boarding house, from which practically no one issued sober, but we had a pile of experience.

15 We began to learn the game, and after our withdrawing from the Oxford Group — oh, a year and a half from the time I sobered, in '34 — we began to hold meetings of the few outside the house who had sobered up. I suppose that was really the first AA meeting. The book hadn't yet been written. We didn't even call it Alcoholics Anonymous; people asked us who we were, and we said, "Well, we're a nameless bunch of alcoholics." I suppose the use of that word "nameless" sort of led us to the idea of anonymity, which was later clapped on the book at the time it was titled.

There were great doings in Clinton Street. I remember those meetings down in the parlor so well. Our eager discussion, our hopes, our fears — and our fears were very great. When anyone in those days had been sober a few months and slipped, it was a terrific calamity. I'll never forget the day, a year and a half after he came to stay with us, that Ebby fell over, and we all said, "Perhaps this is going to happen to all of us." Then, we began to ask ourselves why it was, and some of us pushed on. At Clinton Street, I did most of the talking, but Lois did most of the work, and the cooking, and the loving of those early folks.

Oh my! The episodes that there were! I was away once on a business trip. I'd briefly got back to business. One of them was sleeping on the lounge in the parlor. [Lois] woke up in the middle of the night, hearing a great commotion. He'd got a bottle; he'd also got into the kitchen and had drunk a bottle of maple syrup. This caused great confusion and he had fallen naked into the coal hod, and when Lois opened the door, he asked for a towel to cover up his nakedness.

On another occasion she led this same gentleman through the streets late at night looking for a doctor. And not finding a doctor, then looking for a drink, because, as he said, he could not fly on one wing! And on one occasion, a pair of them were drunk; we had five. And on another occasion, they were all drunk at the same time!

There was the time that two of them began to belabor each other with hunks of two-by-fours down in the basement. And then, poor Ebby, after repeated trials and failures, was finally locked out one night. But low and behold, he appeared anyway because he had come through the coal chute and up the stairs, very much begrimed.

So you see Clinton Street, in a sense, was our little church. It was a kind of blacksmith shop, in which we were hammering away at these principles. It was a hospital and a free boarding house and, of course, for Lois and me, all roads lead back to Clinton Street. And that is particularly true of this group.

It was in 1937, while we were still there, that we got an idea that could spread AA. We would have to have some sort of literature — guide rails for it to run on so it couldn't get garbled. We were still toying with the idea that we had to have paid workers who would be sent to other communities. We thought we'd have to go into the hospital business. Out in Akron, where we had started the first group, they had a meeting and nominated me to come to New York and do all these things.

We were still living at Clinton Street and while we were there we solicited Mr. Rockefeller [John D. Rockefeller Jr.] and some of his friends, who gave us their friendship but, luckily, not much of their money. They gave Smithy [Dr. Bob] and me a little boost during the year of 1938, and that was all. They forced us to stand on our own.

In 1938, Clinton Street saw the beginning of the preparation of the book *Alcoholics Anonymous.* The early chapters of that were written — oh, I should think — about May 1938. Then, we tried to raise money to get the thing published, and we actually sold stock to the local drunks, in this book, not yet written, which is an all-time high for promotions!

Clinton Street also saw, on its second floor, in the bedroom, the writing of the Twelve Steps. We had got to chapter five in the book, and it looked like we would have to say at some point what the book was all about. So I remember lying there on the bed one night, and I was in one of my typical depressive snits, and I had an imaginary ulcer attack.

The drunks who were supposed to be contributing, so that we could eat while the book was being written, were slow on the contributions. You've heard the story since, and I was in a damn bad frame of mind.

16 I lay there with a pad and pencil, and I began to think over these six steps that I've just recited to you, and said I to myself, "Well, if we put down these six steps, the chunks are too big. They'll have to digest too much all at once. Besides, they can wiggle out from in between, and if we're going to do a book, we ought to break those up into smaller pieces."

So I began to write, and in about a half an hour, I think, I had busted them up into smaller pieces. I was rather pleasantly surprised that, when numbered, they added up to twelve — that's significant, very nice.

At this point, a couple of drunks sailed in. I showed them the proposed Twelve Steps, and I caught fits. Why did we need twelve when six were doing fine? And what did I mean by dragging God from the bottom of the list up to the top? Meanwhile, the meetings in the front parlor had largely turned into hassles over the chapters of the book. The roughs were submitted and read at every meeting, so that when the Twelve Steps were proposed, there was a still greater hassle.

Because I'd had this very sudden experience and was on the pious side, I'd lauded these Steps very heavily with the word "God." Other people began to say, "This won't do at all. The reader at a distance is just going to get scared off. And what about agnostic folks like us?" There was another terrific hassle, which resulted in this terrific ten-strike we had: calling God (as you understand Him) the "Higher Power," making a hoop big enough so that the whole world of alcoholics can walk through it.

So, actually, those people who suppose that the elders of AA were going around in white robes surrounded by a blue light, full of virtue, are quite mistaken. I merely became the umpire of the immense amount of hassling that went into the preparation of the AA book, and that took place at Clinton Street. Well, of course, the book was the summit of all our hopes at the time. Along with the hassling, there was an immense enthusiasm. We tried to envision distant readers picking it up and perhaps writing in, perhaps getting sober. Could they do it on the book?

All of those things we speculated on very happily. Finally, in the spring of 1939, the book was ready. We'd made a pre-publication copy of it; it had got by the Catholic Committee on Publications. We'd shown it to all sorts of people; we had made corrections. We had five thousand copies printed, thinking that would be just a mere trifle — that the book would soon be selling millions of copies.

Oh, we were very enthusiastic, us promoters. The *Reader's Digest* had promised to print a piece about the book, and we just saw those books going out in carloads. Nothing of the sort happened. The *Digest* turned us down flat. The drunks had been throwing their money into all this. There were hardly a hundred members in AA — Akron, Cleveland, New York City, sprinkling down around Washington and Philadelphia — and here the thing had utterly collapsed.

At this juncture, the meeting, the first meeting of the Manhattan Group, which really took place in Brooklyn, stopped. And it stopped for a very good reason. That was that the landlord set Lois and me out into the street, and we didn't even have money to move our stuff into storage. Even that and the moving van — that was done on the cuff.

Well, it was then the spring of 1939. Temporarily, the Manhattan Group moved to Jersey; it hadn't got to Manhattan yet. A great friend, Horace C., let Lois and me have a camp belonging to himself and his mother, out at Green Pond. My partner in the book enterprise, old Hank P., now gone, lived at Upper Montclair.

We used to come down to 75 William Street, where we had the little office in which a good deal of the book was actually done. Sundays that summer, we'd come down to Hank's house, where we had meetings which old-timers (just a handful now in Jersey) can remember. Someone lent us a car and they began passing the hat. The Alcoholic Foundation, still completely empty of money, did have one small account called the "Lois B. Wilson Improvement Fund." This improvement fund was fortified every month by a passing of the hat, so that we had the summer camp, we had fifty bucks a month, and someone else lent us a car to try to revive the book *Alcoholics Anonymous* and the flagging movement.

So that summer, meetings were held at Hank's house in Upper Montclair. I think then, for the first time, the Manhattan Group moved to Manhattan. In the fall of that year, when it got cold up there at the summer camp, we moved down to Bob V.'s — he and Mag many of you know, old-timers over in Jersey.

We were close by the Rockland asylum. Bob and I and others went in there, and we started the first institutional group, and several wonderful characters were pried out of there. I hope old Tom M. is here tonight. Tom came over to the V.s' where he had holed up with Lois and me; then put in a room called "Siberia," because it was so cold. We bought a coal stove for four dollars and kept ourselves warm there during the winter.

So did a wonderful alcoholic by the name of Jimmy. He never made good. Jimmy was one of the devious types, and one of our first remarkable experiences with Jimmy was this. When we moved from Green Pond, we brought Marty with us, who had been visiting.[44] And she suddenly developed terrible pains in her stomach. This gentleman, Jimmy, called himself a doctor. In fact, he had persuaded the authorities at Rockland that he was a wonderful physician. They gave him full access to the place. He had keys to all the surgical instruments and, incidentally, I think he had keys to all the pill closets over there.

Marty was suffering awful agonies, and he [Jimmy] said, "Well, there's nothing to it, my dear. You've got gallstones." So he goes over to Rockland. He gets himself some kind of fishing gadget that they put down gullets to fish around in there, and he fishes around and yanks up a flock of gallstones, and she hasn't had a bit of trouble since. And, dear people, it was only years later that we learned the guy wasn't a doctor at all.

Meanwhile, though, the folks over here started a meeting in Bert T.'s tailor shop. Good old Bert is the guy who hocked his then-failing business to save the book *Alcoholics Anonymous* in 1939.

In the fall, he still had the shop, and we began to hold meetings there. Little by little, things began to grow. We went from there to a room in Steinway Hall, and we felt we were in very classic and good company that gave us an aura of respectability, as I remember.

Finally, some of the boys, notably Bert and Horace, said, "AA should have a home. We really ought to have a club." And so the old 24th Street Club, which had belonged to the artists and illustrators and before that was a barn going back to Revolutionary times, was taken over. I think Bert and Horace signed the first lease. They soon incorporated it, though, lest somebody slip on a banana peel outside. Lois and I, who had moved from the V.s' to live with another AA, then decided we wanted a home for ourselves, and we found a single room down in a basement on Barrow Street in Greenwich Village.

I remember Lois and I going through Grand Central wondering where we'd light next, just before the Greenwich Village move. We were very tired that day, and we walked off the main floor there and sat on one of those gorgeous marble stairways leading up to the balcony, and we both began to cry and say, "Where will we ever light? Will we ever have a home?"

Well, we had one for a while in Barrow Street. And when the club was opened up, we moved into one of those rooms there. Tom M. came over from the Vs', and right then and there a Tradition of Alcoholics Anonymous was generated.

It seemed that volunteers had been sweeping out the club. It seemed that many of the alcoholics had keys to the club, and they came and went and sometimes stayed. And sometimes they got drunk and acted very badly — doing we know not what. There had to be somebody there to really look after the place. So we thought we'd approach Old Tom, who had a pension as a fireman.

So we approached Old Tom and we said, "Tom, how would you like to come and live at the club?"

Tom says, "What's on your mind?"

"Well," we said, "we really need somebody here all the time, you know, to make the coffee and see that the place is heated and throw some coal on that furnace over there and lead the drunks outside if they're too bad."

"Ain't ya gonna pay me?" Tom says.

"Oh, no," we said. "This is Alcoholics Anonymous. We can't have any professionals."

Tom says, "I do my Twelfth Step work; I don't charge 'em nothing. But what you guys want is a janitor, and if you're going to get me, you're going to pay, see?"

We were very much disturbed about our own situation. We weren't exactly paid — they were just passing the hat for us, you understand. In fact, I think that we went for seven years of the history of this society with an average income of seventeen hundred bucks a year, which, for a former stockbroker, is not too big.

So this question of who is a professional and who wasn't bore very heavily at the time on Tom and me. And Tom began to get it settled. He began to show that if a special service was asked from anybody full-time, we'd have to pay or not get it. So, finally, we haggled Tom down on the theory that he already had a pension, and he came to live there. So Tom and Lois and I lived there and meetings began in that old club.

That old club saw many a terrific development, and from
that club sprang all the groups in this area. The club saw the passage of the Rockefeller dinner, when we thought we'd all be rich
as a movement, and Mr. Rockefeller saved us by not giving us
money.

The club saw the *Saturday Evening Post* article published. In
fact, the *Post* at that time said, "No pictures, no article." So if you
will look up the March 1, 1941, issue of the *Saturday Post,* you will
see a picture of the interior of the club and a flock of us sitting
before the fire. They didn't use our names, but they insisted on
pictures. Anonymity wasn't then quite what it is today, and with
the advent of that piece, there was a prodigious rush of inquiries — about six thousand of them.

By this time, we'd moved the little office from Newark, New
Jersey, over to Vesey Street. You will find in the old edition of
the book "Box 658, Church Street Annex." And that was the box
into which the first inquiries came. We picked out that loca-
tion because Lois and I were drifters, and we picked it because
it was the center of the geographical area here. We didn't know
whether we'd light in Long Island, New Jersey, or Westchester,
so the first AA post office box was down there with a little office
alongside of it.

The volunteers couldn't cope with this tremendous flock of
inquiries — heartbreakers — but six thousand of them! We simply
had to hire some help. At that point, we asked you people if you'd
send the foundation a buck apiece a year, so we wouldn't have
to throw that stuff in the wastebasket. And that was the beginning of the service office and the book company. That club saw all
those things transpire.[45]

Throughout this talk Bill introduced some memories that
he rarely discussed and gave some wonderful details about the
times-gone-by. Try to imagine how he and Lois must have felt
that day while sitting at Grand Central Station tearfully wondering where their next home would be. Think how difficult it is
for the average alcoholic to find and continue sobriety during

the challenging days of early recovery. Then think of Lois and Bill—their story is truly remarkable! The enormity of what Bill and Lois were going through—having already ministered to hundreds of alcoholics and their families, having written the book (*Alcoholics Anonymous*), and having been left homeless and not knowing where they would land next and for how long—is incomprehensible.

I've heard it said that "character is doing the right thing, even when it costs more than you want to pay." Unquestionably, Bill and Lois displayed exceptional character as they trudged the uncertain road of "happy destiny"—somehow finding the strength and courage not only to endure their personal challenges, but also to overcome the enormous obstacles set before them with the development of AA.

In that same 1955 address to the Manhattan Group, Lois spoke to the crowd and shared the early experience of the Family Groups, which became the Al-Anon Family Groups. Bill then talked about how rapidly Al-Anon was growing.

> Since the St. Louis conference, one new family group has started every single day of the week, someplace in the world. I think the deeper meaning of all this is that AA is something more than a quest for sobriety, because we cannot have sobriety unless we solve the problem of life, which is essentially the problem of living and working together. And the Family Groups are filling this enormous twist that has been put on our domestic relations by our drinking. I think it's one of the greatest things that's happened in years.

Bill had great admiration for Al-Anon and family recovery. He always made it a point to reach out to the family members and encourage Al-Anon. He was, without question, Al-Anon's biggest fan and supporter. It was at his recommendation that Lois and Ann B. began organizing the Family Groups.

He continued addressing the audience with these comments.

Well, let's cut back to old 24th Street. One more thing happened there: a tradition was generated. It had to do with money. You know how slow I was on coming up with that dollar bill tonight? I suppose I was thinking back — some sort of unconscious reflex.

But even then we had a deuce of a time getting that club supported, just passing the hat, no fees, no dues, just the way it should be. But the "no fees and dues" business was construed into no money at all; let "George" do it. I remember I'd been, on this particular day, down to the foundation office [today known as the AA General Service Office], and we'd just put out this dollar-a-year measuring stick for the alcoholics to send us some money if they felt like it. Not too many were feeling like it, and I remember that I was walking up and down the office damning these drunks.

That evening, still feeling sore about the stinginess of the drunks, I sat on the stairs at the old 24th Street Club, talking to some would-be convert. Tom B. was leading the meeting that night, and at the intermission he put on a real plug for money, the first one that I'd ever heard. At that time, money and spirituality couldn't mix, even in the hat. I mean, you mustn't talk about money! Very reluctantly, we'd gone into the subject with Tom M. [the caretaker] and the landlord. We were behind in the rent.

Well, Tom put on that heavy pitch, and I went on talking to my prospect, and as the hat came up the stairs, and as it came along, I fished in my pocket and pulled out half a buck. That very day, I think, Ebby had come in the office a little the worse for wear; and with a very big heart, I had handed him five dollars. Our total income at that time was thirty bucks a week, which had come out of the Rockefeller dinner affair; so I'd given him five bucks of the thirty and felt very generous, you see.

But now comes the hat to pay for the light and heat and so forth — rent — and I pull out this half dollar and I look absent-mindedly at it, and I put my hand in the other pocket and pull out a dime and put it in the hat. So I have never railed at alcoholics for not getting up the money. There, you see, was the beginning of the AA Traditions — things that had to do with professionalism and money.

Following 1941, this thing just mushroomed. Groups began to break off out into the suburbs. But a lot of us still wanted a club, and the 24th Street Club just wouldn't do the trick. We got an offer from Norman Vincent Peale to take over a church at 41st Street. The church was in a neighborhood that had deteriorated sadly. It was said to be a rather sinful neighborhood, if you gather what I mean. The last young preacher that Peale had sent there seemed very much against drinking and smoking and other even more popular forms of sin; therefore, he had no parishioners.

Here was this tremendous church, and all that we could see was a bigger and bigger club in New York City. So we moved in. The body of the church would hold one thousand people, and we had a hall upstairs that would hold another eight hundred, and we envisioned this as soon full. Then there were bowling alleys downstairs, and we figured the drunks would soon be getting a lot of exercise. After they warmed up down there, they could go upstairs in the gymnasium.

Then, we had cooking apparatus for a restaurant. This was to be our home, and we moved in. Well, sure enough, the place filled up just like mad! Well then, questions of administration, questions of morals, questions of meetings, questions of which was the Manhattan Group and which was the club and which was the Intergroup — the secretary of the club was also the Intergroup secretary — began to get this seething mass into terrific tangles, and we learned a whole lot about clubs!

Whilst all this was going on, the AA groups were spreading all throughout America and to foreign shores. And each group, like our own, was having its terrific headaches. In that violent period, nobody could say whether this thing would hang together or not. Would it simply explode and fly to pieces?

On thousands of anvils of experience, of which the Manhattan Group was certainly one down in that 41st Street Club, more sparks came off that anvil than any I ever saw. We hammered out the Traditions of Alcoholics Anonymous, which were first published in 1945. We hammered out the rudiments of an Intergroup, which now has become one of the best there is anywhere, right here in New York.

Finally, however, the club got so big that it bust. The Intergroup moved out. So did the Manhattan Group, with five thousand dollars, which was its part of the take, which it hung on to like this. And from the Manhattan Group's experience, we learned that, although the foundation needs a reserve, for God's sake, don't have any money in a group treasury! The hassles about that five thousand dollars lasted until they got rid of it somehow.

Then, you all moved down to dear old Sam Shoemaker's Calvary, the very place of our beginning. Now, we've made another move and so we grow, and such has been the road that leads back to the kitchen table at Clinton Street.[46]

chapter eight

The Birth Pangs of AA through Bill and Bob's Early Letters

THE FOLLOWING EXCHANGE OF LETTERS between Bill W. and Dr. Bob enlarges upon the early AA story and provides further insight into the working relationship between the two cofounders. The letters discuss topics such as the Rockefeller Dinner, the writing and publishing of the Big Book, and the general welfare of the cofounders and AA.

In most cases I chose to include the entire document. However, in a few cases I removed more personal information to concentrate on the sections that help tell significant details of Bill and Dr. Bob's story. All the letters can be found in the archives at Stepping Stones, the historic home of Bill and Lois Wilson.

The first letter written by Dr. Bob to Bill was dated September 27, 1937.

> *Awfully glad to hear from you and to learn of your anticipated visit. Hope nothing interferes with your plans. We can easily find room for as many as you want to bring, for as long as you wish.*
>
> *Between Paul, T. Henry, and ourselves we'll have no trouble housing and feeding you and your gang. All our gang is doing OK*

except Phil, who finally ran amuck after 23 months of dryness because he was not willing to do the things he was supposed to do. He had been getting careless and indifferent for the past 5 months but we could not seem to head him off. Am sorry, of course, but I can't make folks do what they are supposed to do.

I have several new ones on fire so the numbers are not decreasing.

Dr. Bob wrote this letter to Bill a few weeks before the famous meeting in Akron where they "counted heads." The meeting was held in the home of T. Henry and Clarace Williams. The count showed forty people who were believed to be sober at the time. Plans were made at that meeting for Bill W. to go back to New York to raise money and begin writing a book.

It's easy to see how "broke" this crowd was at the time, and how Bob wanted to assure Bill that they would be able to accommodate the group from New York. These were challenging times for this yet nameless society, and the "numbers" were important to calculate its strength. Phil, who ran amuck after being *careless and indifferent,* was one of the earliest members of the Akron crowd. It is interesting to note Dr. Bob's comment that Phil "was not willing to do the things he was supposed to do." This was before the AA Big Book had been written and the program was still "word of mouth."

Dr. Bob wrote three more letters to Bill in 1937 after Bill's October visit. In one of them, dated November 22, he wrote the following.

Glad to hear from you again and to learn that some interest is being evidenced by the Foundation. I showed your letter to Paul, T. Henry, and Clarissa [Clarace W.] only. Paul says he thinks he can come to NY on relatively short notice and so do I, at least with a little financial assistance. The trip could have to be a little hasty, perhaps two days in NY (12th & 13th) for I feel that if I go that far east I should spend at least one day with Mother, so we should be gone from here about a week.

The next letter:

11/30/37

Dear Bill,

Great to hear from you and to learn of the Foundation's continued interest. Talked to Paul a few minutes ago. He says he will be very glad to accept your kind invitation, as do I also. So far we know we can be there, but unless you urge it, I shall not bring anyone else besides Paul because I shall ride up to Vermont on my way back here, just a little short-cut I thought up.

Everything is in fair shape here, though not perfect, but I doubt if it ever will be as far as Phil is concerned though I hope I am wrong. We (Paul & I) expect we will leave here early Saturday AM and get to your house sometime in evening if we don't freeze to death in the PA mountains somewhere. Shall certainly be glad to tuck my feet under your table and to be with you and Lois again.

The Foundation Bob mentions was the Rockefeller Foundation. Bill had scheduled a December meeting with people from the Rockefeller Foundation to discuss the possibility of securing funding for AA. Bill and Dr. Bob felt that a great deal of money was needed to get the program off the ground and enable them to carry the message quickly. The meeting was attended by Bill, Dr. Silkworth, Dr. Bob, Paul S., and several New York members and members of John D. Rockefeller's staff and Rockefeller Foundation board members. One result of the meeting was that Frank Amos of the foundation went to Akron to see what he could learn about Dr. Bob and the group there. The result of this meeting proved to be, perhaps, one of the key factors in AA's survival: the realization that too much money could ruin it.

The following is another letter written by Dr. Bob.

February 17, 1938

Dear Bill,

We had a delightful visit from Mr. Amos as L. may have told you by this time. He was here Friday night and Saturday. . . . He returned Monday PM late, had dinner at T. Henry and Clarissa's [Clarace's]. In the evening about 50–60 of the men and their wives gathered so he could see and talk with them. Tuesday he had a chance to check up on me and see some business possibilities. I had lunch with him on Tuesday and also dinner. He seemed very favorably impressed. If he were not, I certainly do not know what we could do to impress him. . . . Of course he heard some Oxford Group chatter but we tried to impress him with the fact that as far as the alcoholic setup was concerned we could not be identified with the group and explained why such a setup was impossible. I think he understands things OK.

These letters follow the documented AA history. The aa.org website timeline explains it this way.

Frank Amos, who attended the December meeting and is a close friend of John D. Rockefeller, Jr., agrees to assess the Akron group and explore the possibility of opening a small hospital for alcoholics. In February 1938 he spends several days in the city. Impressed by the recovery rate of Akron group members, he proposes a recuperative facility to be run by Dr. Bob. To Rockefeller he recommends a sum of $50,000 for the early work, but Rockefeller thinks the Fellowship should be self-supporting. The philanthropist does, however, contribute $5,000 toward Bill and Dr. Bob's basic needs.

Dr. Bob also mentions "the Oxford Group chatter" in his letter and says, "As far as the alcoholic setup was concerned we could not be identified with the group." Here we see that AA (still a nameless group) had already pulled away from the Oxford Group. Dr. Bob continued to attend meetings until 1940, according to his own words. But from this letter we can see that he wanted to draw the distinction between the two groups and keep the alcoholic setup separate.

I was able to locate a letter that Bill wrote in the late spring or early summer of 1938. The letter is undated.

Dear Bob:

I have been remiss, but there have been reasons. After getting home from Akron I had about concluded to let the book idea lie quiet while people thought it over. I found, however, that a lot of people, including Frank Amos, had got quite afire. Frank thought something ought to be started right away. I told him that you people had only just begun to consider the matter and pointed out at length the dangers and difficulties of such a venture: particularly our fear of undesirable publicity. Considering the rate at which we grow, he, and others including myself, began to think that publicity would come anyhow. Why then not our own anonymous view of ourselves, thus precluding the possibility that someone else garbled the situation before we had a chance to say anything. Thus we came to the conclusion that in a tentative way a beginning should be made. In this fashion, having some definite proposals laid out and some writing done, we would have a concrete basis for discussion.

As a starting point I have, with the help of the folks here, dictated and mimeographed two chapters of the proposed book, one in the nature of an introduction and the second my own story. These I enclose to you together with a rough outline of the contents of other chapters.

I imagine you could use this material as a sort of trial balloon, and a starting point for discussion of what you folks out there believe the book ought to contain. Although I have made the beginning, I feel that the completed book should represent the work of many people; particularly the individual stories, which I think should be as little edited as possible. They will naturally be the heart of the book and must represent the feelings, experiences, and personalities of those who write them. As you will note, the chapter outline calls for nine stories of a chapter each, of about the same length as my own. My feeling is that Anne should do the one portraying the wife of an alcoholic. We have here a very striking story in the person of Florence Rankin who is an alcoholic and also the wife of an alcoholic. She has been alright for about nine months and has a very unusual and powerful witness. It may be that like Anne, she should have a chapter to herself. Then we might, beginning with myself, take seven of us in consecutive order, omitting any who have fallen from grace. The story of a fellow like Ernie would be omitted from this series, but could be included in the shorter narrative or perhaps, considering his wonderful comeback, with powerful effect in the chapter on failures. It is thought each of these nine chapters should run about five thousand words. Then we might have five chapters, each consisting of five witnesses of about one thousand words each, elected mostly, I should think, consecutively, except for some especially striking case, and the witnesses of a couple of beginners.

The foregoing are suggestions only. We can never tell where the next best idea may come from and who will make a still better suggestion. So please take the picture I have sketched and do not hesitate to add, subtract or multiply it in any way which occurs to you all. I am not suffering at the moment from any pride of authorship, so let everyone do their best and, if they like, their worst.

It might be a good idea if you showed this stuff around generally, and then asked people to write their own stories in their own language and at all the length they want: covering those experiences from childhood up, which illustrate the salient points of their character. Probably emphasis should be placed on those qualities and actions which caused them to come into collision with their fellows and those things which lay beneath the tendency to excessive drinking; the queer state of mind and emotion preceding the first drink. The first medical attention required. The various institutions visited; these ought to be brought in. There ought to be a description of the man's feelings as he met our crowd, his first sense of God being with him, his feeling of hopelessness and now his sense of victory, his application of principles to his everyday life, including domestic, business, and relations with other alcoholics; the release he gets from working with others, the victories God has given him, the problems which still face him, and his progress with them; these are other possible points. When this is done we can sit down with these authors, one at a time, and fit their story into the pattern of the book. Everyone should write with feeling, not laying it on too thick. However, and above all let's not try to be too literary. It will be much better to be guided.

I can't say how soon I shall get to Akron, for we are in the throes of raising more money to carry on with. But if you could get the ball rolling along these lines, it would be great. This would much greatly facilitate tying up the packages quickly and neatly later on.

Now about money matters: in the first place I am sure we could use quite a bit to carry on the general work for the next year. Situations are bound to arise which will need some under-pinning. Moreover, it is going to take time and money to get this book out and put it into circulation. In this latter connection we are told by Silas Bent that if we can produce a book as useful and as moving as the first two chapters suggest, it may have a very large sale. You will remember Silas as an alcoholic we worked with out here. He is a star reporter and writer, and was at one time editor of the New York Times Sunday magazine. He thoroughly knows all the ropes we shall need, and offers his services as an editor or as a writer, if we so desire. He thinks that prior to the publication of the book, articles based upon it should be published in the Reader's Digest, Saturday Evening Post, etc. or perhaps some of the chapters of the book itself. This would ensure a very large sale of the volume, if it is any good. We think we can get some of the life insurance companies to recommend it in their advertising that people read the book. By the way, you might all be thinking up a good title. Nearly everyone agrees that we should sign the volume,

Alcoholics Anonymous. Titles such as "Haven, One Hundred Men, Comes the Dawn," etc. have been suggested.

What would you think about the formation of a charitable corporation to be called, let us say, "Alcoholics Anonymous"? Money coming in from the book could be handled through it as well as any funds arising from contributions by corporations benefited by our work. We should always remember that perhaps someday our activities will be scrutinized by hostile microscopes with the idea of proving we are a racket. If we now form a corporation whose control is exercised by a board composed largely of disinterested and nonalcoholic people, we shall have closed the door to such criticism. The trustees of this corporation could administer any other enterprises we might want to engage in: such as, for instance, sanitariums.

It is expected that we can obtain from friends of Frank Amos suitable "To whom it may concern" letters, introducing us to people of means. The plan is to approach such people saying that we need funds to carry on our general work and to publish this book. They will be shown chapters of the book and will be told that we intend to become self-supporting within one year, but that we shall need financial assistance in the meantime. So we are hard at work in the money department out here and I have no doubt that we shall raise what we need. When this is accomplished some of us will probably come out for a visit at which time we can develop matters further.

Meanwhile, salutations to the alcoholic brethren and God be with you all!

Much yours,

Bill

P.S. I believe Frank Amos concurs — Let us know what you think.

Bill spells out the exact state of affairs and his thoughts about the book very clearly in this letter. There was still concern about immediate money, and of course he wanted Dr. Bob's input. Although later, Bill would refer to himself as the chief promoter, this letter appears to be from a man who wanted to involve others and wasn't interested in taking the credit.

Bill's next letter was dated September 20, 1939.

Dear Smithie,

As you probably know, the blast in Liberty *is out, perhaps not all that could be desired, but good for such a publication. Hope it will stir things up a bit, particularly in the neighborhood of 30 Rockefeller Plaza.*

I dropped in there yesterday and found that Mr. Richardson commenced to push the firm of Pierce & Hendrick, a money raising organization with which he is well acquainted, for some immediate results. They are about to send out an appeal for money to a selected list. I imagine this will take time but it shows they really mean to do something. They do not wish to push Mr. R. at this time, preferring to further build up enthusiasm among the people who surround him, such as Harry Emerson Fosdick and his brother Raymond Fosdick, head of the Rockefeller Foundation. It turns out that the latter is a friend and former business associate of Bob V., one of our crowd who is doing exceptionally good work. Bob is going to see Raymond Fosdick and try for a definite yes or no.

Meanwhile I am starting an approach to the Guggenheim Foundation thinking perhaps a fellowship can be secured by you. I am taking the enclosed letter in there with the book and some other material as soon as possible, trying, of course, to secure a proper introduction if I can. Your situation is clearly within their province and powers and I hope they will be favorably disposed. It is probable that this approach will tend to hurry up matters at 30 Rockefeller Plaza as I have discussed the Guggenheim situation with Messrs. Chipman, Richardson, and Amos, who are willing that we give it a whirl.

Thanks so much for your comforting and cheering letter. After all, we cannot do much ourselves for other people except to present them with an opportunity; the opportunity to feel the Presence and know the power and love of the Father of Lights. These slips are a great deal like murder or arson — they get well advertised, but many of the brethren here are having no trouble at all and most of them are happily working with others like the very devil.

We are growing at an alarming rate though I have no further fear of large numbers. It is simply a question of presenting them with an opportunity which they accept at once, or else fall back on what we call out here "The Bottle Heat Treatment," which is often quite effective when that therapy is thoroughly applied. Far from being gloomy we remain enthusiastic as can be. Everywhere there is a spirit and absence of friction, which is mighty cheering to me. After all, the main thing is that these people are finding God and getting well and I often wonder why I am so concerned at times over my own personal welfare. It should be enough that one can be a little useful rather than function as cemetery fertilizer.

So, cheerio, Smithie — God bless you and Annie and everybody.

Bill touches on several interesting topics in this letter. The *Liberty* article was dated for September 30, yet he mentions it already being out. *Liberty* was a weekly publication so it's unlikely that it had already been released, although in Canada the article appeared in the September 16 issue.

It's also apparent that both Dr. Bob and Bill were still working hard to secure funding. By this time, the Big Book had been published, and Bill and Lois had been evicted from their Brooklyn home.

Another interesting thing to note here is Bill's statement about presenting "the opportunity to feel the Presence and know the power and love of the Father of Lights." This description, coming from Bill, gives great insight into how he personally felt about what the AA program offers to the willing alcoholic. Surely his own spiritual experience was the basis of his choice of words.

Overall, the letter seems intended to offer some reassurance to Dr. Bob that things were going well.

Two months later, Bill sent this letter dated December 4, 1939.

Dear Bob,

We got back safely from a visit to you people which was so wonderful in so many ways. So once more, thanks for the hospitality and especially your suits — I don't know what I'd have done without them.

The book is moving out at a good clip and plenty of inquiries are in. Fitz M. has just come from Washington with good reports from that section. Some of us who are free to move about are going down soon to lend a hand.

Now about 30 Rockefeller Plaza. Progress continues smooth and sure, but when anything definite will happen, I can't say. The boss over there has read the book, asked a pile of questions, and has written enthusiastically to a friend. Whether to give a large dinner for those who might be interested in us, whether to go quietly to a few friends, or whether to do this thing entirely himself at the beginning, the gentleman is not sure. But he has given Mr. Richardson to understand that something will be done and that something pretty soon. He has a lot of year-end meetings and is now out of town visiting his pet project at Williamsburg, VA. So Mr. Richardson feels that it will not be until sometime in January that action will be taken.

While we were visiting you, the New York boys held a business meeting to which they invited Mr. Richardson. At this meeting they signed a petition asking me to continue full time in the work if I could. It was on this occasion that Mr. Richardson told them that something would surely be forthcoming at least to the extent of providing an office, some expense money, and a few workers.

Like yourself we are growing at a phenomenal rate.

By early 1940, things were really buzzing. AA was taking on large numbers of members resulting from the *Liberty Magazine* article and a series of articles written by Elrick Davis and published in the *Cleveland Plain Dealer* in October and November of 1939.

In January 1940, Bill wrote a letter to Dr. Bob and followed it with three more in the same month. Because of its historically significant information, the entire first letter is included here.

1/8/40

Dear Smithy:

Now and then I get a whisper from out your way to the effect that, spiritually speaking, "Life is Abundant." I am led to believe that God is very good indeed but His boundless wisdom still keeps thumbs down on oversupplying material manna.

The manna shortage down here is still acute. Just when this old and grievous form of vitamin deficiency will be repaired I still can't say. In fact, I've gotten used to it that I wouldn't know how to set if things were different. People are continuing to get well which is, I suppose, the main thing, and my happiness about it is very great. The boys chipped in and saved my goods on which no storage had ever been paid and there are enough frogskins to last a week or so — and so much for that. We seem to be holed up at Bob V.'s for the winter. As I think you know, he has a very large house with an unused addition, into which we have moved bag and baggage. We have the best coal stove in New York state, all for the price of $4.00, and one of the brethren who is not using his car has turned it over to us.

Meanwhile, I am in close touch with 30 Rockefeller Plaza where there is more insistence than ever that something is going to be done this month. Dr. Blaisdell, head of the large state institution at Rockland, New York is raising his voice quite loudly on our behalf both at Rockefeller Center and elsewhere. He promises to be a great friend and has just sent a stenographic record of an address made before the Board of Visitors of his institution to the authorities at Albany.

He has provided a bus by which students of Alcoholics Anonymous may be transported to our Sunday classes. Ten speakers of truth have already graduated from his place, and upon our recommendation, he is about to let out twenty more. It looks as though more than half of these people will permanently recover, which from Dr. Blaisdell's point of view would be miraculous. Careful case records are being kept of those who are exposed to our notions and one of his assistants will soon prepare a medical paper on the results to date.

Dr. Fredrick is also starting to consult us about his difficulties with alcoholics and just turned over a prospect the other day.

Am interested to learn that meetings are being held at your house. In the name of Heaven, where do you put eighty people? We are using the South Orange Community house for Jersey social meeting during the wintertime, and expect to make similar arrangement at Greenwich House, New York City for Sunday gatherings. Tuesday meetings are still held at Steinway Hall, but we are looking around for something larger and more suitable.

Fitz M. ran across T. Henry and Clarissa [Clarace] *at Calvary where they were morally rearming. I went to visit them at once, but they had gone. Am curious to know what happened out there in Akron. As I recall the arrangement, meetings were to be held on Wednesdays as usual strictly free from denominational or Oxford group bias, and that Saturday night had been set aside for those who wished to identify themselves with M.R.A.* [Moral Re-Armament].

Ruth got a letter from the S.'s [surname removed here for anonymity] *saying that the shift to your house has wonderfully cleared the air. For this I am truly grateful, especially for Annie and your sake, for if we be poor we ought to at least be permitted to live in peace and serenity.*

Lois is grand — never in better shape — and I am especially glad to report the same of Hank who while still short of manna is in the best spiritual form I have ever seen him. I do not think he would mind if I took you into our confidence about [the] future status of the book and the Works Publishing Company.

We have both concluded to turn our entire interest over to the Alcoholic Foundation lock, stock, and barrel, no strings attached. This may be done this month or as soon as we can get enough money together to incorporate Works Publishing Company. Though the donation will be made without any restrictions upon it we plan to write the trustees a joint letter to the effect that some of us, and for one, a certain Dr. Smith, have put a great deal of time and money into the Alcoholics Anonymous project; that we all have people dependent upon us; that we hope the trustees will take notice from time to time the needs of our wives and families; but that in any event such income as may grow from the book, either as royalties or dividends, is completely under the control of the trustees of the Alcoholic Foundation. Hank and I would rather you said nothing of this arrangement for the present, except perhaps to Clarence and Dorothy S. This arrangement ought to remove the last vestige of criticism about the book millionaires.

Hope we can get out to see you soon. I am still a director of that concern at Anderson, Indiana, and may have to make a trip sometime this month to that place. Hope I'll have enough extra carfare to take in all the midwest "Anonymi."

Lois and I have remarked many times that our last visit was the finest ever had though I am almost sure we never have thanked you for everything.

So God bless all the brethren, and our Annie and Smithy.

Until then.

By 1940, the Oxford Group had taken the name "Moral Re-Armament." The meetings of the New York group were still being held at Calvary House, which was part of Calvary Church where Sam Shoemaker was rector. Evidently, T. Henry and Clarace Williams, members of the Oxford Group in Akron, had visited Calvary for moral rearming.

Another interesting item is that meetings were being held at Dr. Bob's house with eighty people present. It can be very tricky to make claims of membership totals in an anonymous organization. The foreword to the second edition Big Book (1955) states, "By the end of 1939 it was estimated that 800 alcoholics were on their way to recovery." It was also estimated that some five hundred people inquired about AA as the result of the *Plain Dealer* articles. This answers questions about where the people came from to attend the meetings at Dr. Bob's.

In Bill's next letter he discusses member totals that are quite different than the estimates in the second edition publication. Certainly, as time passed AA improved its tracking of early members, which could account for the higher numbers published in 1955.

Jan. 10, 1940

Dear Doc:

Now the deluge:

Since writing you yesterday things have happened fast. I found a telegram in our box from Dorothy Giles, a well known feature writer, who has specialized in popular presentations of metaphysical, physiological, and spiritual topics. I called on her and she tells me she has a commission, or what amounts to one, from the Reader's Digest *to do a special article. Though they turned us down a few weeks ago, they now seem in a devil of a rush and tell her they are willing to postpone the deadline on what I suppose to be their March issue if she will step on it and get a piece done.*

She and I spent twelve hours together yesterday, during which time she took in a Steinway Hall meeting, sitting around in a restaurant with the gang for hours afterward. The rest of the night she spent in preparing an outline for an article to be submitted to the Digest today. If they accept she will immediately run off a rough draft, submitting if for criticism, comment, or deletion. If time does not permit, I'll send a wire a few hours in advance as to when I can talk to you on the telephone about any questionable point.

She has not yet indicated just what form her narrative will take, but thinks in a general way, that she will do a reportorial piece emphasizing the usefulness of the work to the community and its human element. The main objective of the article will be to authenticate our work beyond question to alcoholics, their families, doctors, ministers, and so far as possible to the general public.

I have requested her to make it evident that the work in the middle west has progressed faster and better and I think it is her intention to build her picture mostly around the Akron-Cleveland situation. She is going to be very careful to avoid overstatement so that when a detailed investigation is sometime made we shall not have exaggerated anything.

In our long conversation I covered the A.A. situation from the religious, medical, social, personal, and historical angle. To say the least, she got an earful. Of course, I didn't try to tell her in any way what to write except that we would like emphasis on Cleveland and Akron.

I am quite sure she would like to mention the story of the barber from Orrville and what has since happened in the community, though of course she won't mention such a small town by name, although I see no objection to using such names as Cleveland, Akron, New York, Chicago, Los Angeles, San Francisco, etc. In telling her our story I noted that since you were a doctor you might object to being pointed out as an Akron physician in the article. She said she would gladly disguise the situation if you still so decided, though since the Beacon-Journal article I wasn't sure how you would like yourself to appear. Will you let me know airmail?

I told her I thought that ten people had recovered in Orrville as a result of that visit to you two years ago (?). Will you check how many of them there are now and how long ago the original conversation took place, and how many of the boys have kept their noses fairly clean.

I am so anxious that the Digest article be impeccably factual that it's too bad we haven't a detailed record of the total results to date. Though Miss Giles does not care for much in the way of statistics, she did ask for an approximation rather than an overstatement.

After thinking the matter over carefully, I have just mailed her a statement to this effect, which I am sure is ultra-conservative — "approximately 400 alcoholics, men and women, are now actively interested in Alcoholics Anonymous. These members have been identified with the work for periods ranging from five years to a few months. Of these, about two hundred have had no relapse. Roughly 100 have had some difficulty, but in the opinion of the group will recover. Because of their lack of interest or mental condition, the remainder are questionable."

I am making allowance for the fact that the western results are somewhat better than ours here in the east, so I would like to know if you think the foregoing approximation is a fair one. I have stated our membership at 400 counting the western department at 275, including Chicago, Detroit, and outlaying. I have put ourselves down for 125 though the total is actually more like 200. I'm quite sure a careful survey would show close to 500 interested participants.

So let me have any comments or useful facts you have right now and I'll give you ample notice by wire if it's necessary to phone.

Immediately drew this situation to the attention of 30 Rockefeller Plaza, quoting Miss Giles to the effect that if the Liberty article produced inquiries by the hundred, the Digest would produce them by the thousand. They said, "Go right ahead," this somewhat to my surprise, for it surely must mean they plan to get up the necessary when the brethren show up. Here's hoping!

Best to all.

Less than a week later Bill followed up on the progress of the proposed *Digest* piece by writing Bob this note.

Jan. 16, 1940

Dear Doc:

Received your letter and wire OK but had not seen either at the time the rough draft was sent off to you. In fact, I did not see some of the rough draft myself.

Just phoned Miss Giles who said she told the Digest that time must be allowed to check the article with you and the Foundation Trustees so no serious error should creep into it.

When interviewed by her I was requested to tell the whole story in consecutive order at great length. Upon finishing I told her I did not know to what extent you wanted to be brought in personally so she had to guess at that in the rough draft. I did, however, feel that strong emphasis should be placed on the general situation in the mid-west where the work is larger and more successful than here.

She said that idea would be approved by the Digest as people are not interested throughout the country in what goes on in New York City. I also explained the Oxford Group origin of some of our ideas and there was quite a lot of discussion of spiritual experience during which I described my own. She came to the Steinway meeting that evening where she picked up more material, some of which she has used.

*According to her, the Digest is very exacting about an article
of this kind. They are very gun-shy on religion and perhaps
more-so on the Oxford Group. Therefore, she could not present
a description with too much religious or O.G. emphasis. Neither
could she slant the article directly to those who know the alcoholic
problem. The article has to be of wide reader interest. She felt that
the most she could do in such a piece would be to arouse curiosity
in a way pleasing to the general reader and absolutely assure
him that our methods, whatever they are, do work. She said she
would have to present the article from the reporter's standpoint,
meaning that neither she nor the Digest could be placed in a
position of siding with us. She merely would try to report what she
saw and heard.*

*To the part of the draft I saw there were several objections which
I made clear to her. In the first place I did not think there was
enough emphasis on the western situation and far too much upon
the part I had played personally. Moreover, the idea that the
whole scheme was a sudden conception or revelation coming to
me was inaccurate.*

*After taking stock of my objections she said that she could
understand but felt her readers would demand that the article
hang about people and personalities; that a strictly factual
description of a group of people with no emphasis on the
leadership would be too dry for the general reader. She agreed to
tone me down and build the western end up through the middle of
the article, as she had first written the beginning and the end of
it. The middle, referring to you, I did not see before it went to you.*

*By experience I have found that we cannot have exactly what we
want when dealing with newspapers or periodicals. Any piece of
this kind has to be a compromise between what you want and
what the publisher wants. The question always is — how far to
yield to their desires.*

*The principle that I have been trying to bear in mind is that
here is a publication which is the best one in which to convince*

the general public that we have something which is on the level and which works, and something which will convince also the doctor, the minister, the alcoholic, and his family. If these people are not convinced, we cannot reach them, therefore, a fair and factual article, even though it be not the best, is infinitely better than nothing at all. Surely our work has progressed far enough so that we are almost duty bound to let people know of it as soon as we can. Hence, we cannot be too insistent on perfection from our standpoint and get nothing at all. It wouldn't be fair to the thousands who lie sick not knowing how to get well.

I realize that I am assuming a responsibility in this matter for which I haven't sufficient authority. If, therefore, after you have checked to your satisfaction you still feel that this move is untimely or not to the best interests of all, I wish you would let me know.

There is another aspect of the Digest piece which presents an opportunity upon which I am counting heavily, namely that its publication will exert such a pressure on 30 Rockefeller Plaza to do something, that they cannot refuse. I called Mr. Chipman as soon as I knew of the Digest request and he has since told me he wrote a memorandum about it to Mr. R. who again promised to act.

So, Smithy, I am doing my level best in a situation which has its advantages as well as its disadvantages. Please let fly with any suggestions or criticisms, for God knows I feel like I need them.

Yours,

In the next letter Bill discusses the "revised draft" of the proposed *Digest* article and the plans for the "Rockefeller Dinner." Mr. Rockefeller decided to host a special dinner so his friends could learn more about Alcoholics Anonymous. The dinner was held on February 8, 1940, and Dr. Harry Emerson Fosdick, a well-known and respected minister, was the featured speaker.

> **Mr. John D. Rockefeller, Jr.**
> **requests the pleasure of your company**
> **at dinner**
> **on Thursday, the eighth of February**
> **at seven o'clock**
> **The Union Club**
> **Park Avenue and 69th Street**
>
> **Mr. William G. Wilson, author of "Alcoholics Anonymous"**
> **and Dr. Harry Emerson Fosdick**
> **will speak on an effective control of alcoholism**
>
> **R.s.v.p.**
> **30 Rockefeller Plaza**   **Business Suit**

Jan. 23, 1940

Dear Smithy,

Hope you have seen the proposed Digest article by this time.
Dorothy Giles was to have mailed you the revised draft some time
Saturday. She expected to have it done on Friday, but when I saw
her that afternoon she showed me only the first few pages. What I
saw looked very moderate in tone which should be better for us.

Before she started the second attempt I spent some time with her
going over the first one. In fact the particular copy on which you
had made your suggestions. So she certainly knew when she wrote
the second one approximately what way we would like it handled.

Now about the dinner on February 8th. Though Mr. Richardson has
been very casual about it, there seems no doubt that Mr. R. is taking
the whole affair very seriously for he has personally sent invitations
to about 150 prominent men and will himself act as toastmaster at
the affair. The invitation also mentions Dr. Harry Emerson Fosdick
who I suppose will provide the oratory. The invitation, though rather
elegant, specifies that business suits will be worn.

Just what the program is going to be I don't yet know. Mr. Richardson told me that they might make an attempt to raise money for a three year program right at the dinner table, or they might not touch upon the subject so directly until later. Other than these facts I know nothing of their plans, for by earnest request I was relieved somewhat of taking part in the money raising activities.

They would like a few alcoholics to be there but no invitations have been sent to any of us as yet because I first wanted to discuss the matter with you in Akron. Personally I'd like to see Clarence S. and possibly Jack D. come with you though you may have a better idea about that. Jack's name came to mind only for the reason that he is well known to them, has been sober for some time, is employed, and can, if necessary, keep a close mouth.

My trip fell through last week because one of the Pierce-Governor directors was sick. I fully expect to leave New York Thursday, Jan. 25th and come back through Cleveland Monday, Jan. 29th when I can spend a couple of days with you if the scenery isn't shifted meanwhile.

Affectionately,

Bill W. recapped the Rockefeller dinner in the book *Alcoholics Anonymous Comes of Age.*

Nelson Rockefeller. Directly in front of me was Wendell Willkie. The dinner was squab on toast. For a bunch of ex-drunks, we were doing remarkably well. We wondered how Mr. Rockefeller had dared to go so far out on a limb for an obscure and struggling fellowship of alcoholics.

After dinner Mr. Nelson Rockefeller rose to his feet. He expressed his father's regret for being unable to attend. He told how deeply Mr. John D., Jr., had been affected by his experience with this society of Alcoholics Anonymous, promising a highly interesting evening.

Nelson Rockefeller began to introduce the speakers. Dr. Fosdick gave us a most wonderful testimonial and expressed complete confidence in our future. Dr. Kennedy warmly endorsed us and read a letter of protest he had written to the Journal of the American Medical Association *because in their review of the book* Alcoholics Anonymous *they had somewhat ridiculed us. Dr. Bob spoke briefly, and I gave a rapid account of my own experience as a drinker, my recovery, and the subsequent history of our fellowship. As we watched the faces of the guests, it was evident that we had captured their sympathetic interest.*

Great influence and great wealth were soon to be at our disposal. Weariness and worry were to be things of the past. Finally the big moment came. Mr. Nelson Rockefeller, visibly moved, got to his feet once more. On behalf of his father, he thanked us all for coming. He reiterated that few more affecting things than Alcoholics Anonymous *had ever crossed his father's life. His father would be delighted, Nelson said, to know how many guests had availed themselves of the chance to see the beginnings of this most promising adventure of Alcoholics Anonymous.*

Breathlessly we waited for the climax — the matter of money. Nelson Rockefeller obliged us. Continuing, he said, "Gentlemen, you can all see that this is a work of good will. Its power lies in the fact that one member carries the good message to the next, without any thought of financial income or reward. Therefore, it is our belief that Alcoholics Anonymous should be self-supporting so far as money is concerned. It needs only our good will." Whereupon the guests clapped lustily, and after cordial handshakes and good-bys all around, the whole billion dollars' worth of them walked out the door. [47]

By the end of March some tangible results from the dinner were manifesting. This next letter discusses some of those results. Keep in mind as you read these letters that AA's Twelve Traditions had not yet been developed. The Traditions first appeared in the *AA Grapevine* in August 1946. Much of the activity from the late 1930s and early 1940s created the necessity for the Traditions. These letters give a glimpse of intimate goings-on of the rapidly growing fellowship. Both letters transcribed here can be found in their original form in appendix B.

30 Vesey St.,

New York City.

March 29, 1940

Dear Smithy:

Little by little the results of the Union Club dinner are becoming apparent in several ways, not that the Foundation treasury is bulging as it still has only about three thousand dollars. Practically all of the gentlemen who attended the dinner, and quite a lot of those who did not, contributed. There was a large amount of enthusiastic comment and letter writing, but the amount of dough required seemed so small to the gentlemen that each contributed only a little.

A little while ago I got a letter from Mr. Rockefeller expressing great pleasure over the impression AA created at the dinner. Also commending our unselfishness and effort, etc. There is a meeting next Monday to consider ways and means to finish up the job, so I have no doubt that we shall arrive in time at whatever place we are supposed to be going. The number one philanthropist, however, at this writing is Mr. Charles Noyes.

You remember talking with him about his brother the night of the dinner. The brother came to town the other day and Charles set out a really good meal for the three of us at his town house. During the course of the dinner he said we ought to have more local publicity and mentioned a series of articles in the New York World *similar to the* Plain Dealer *series. I remarked that before doing anything like that we had to have a local headquarters of some seating capacity with office and club arrangements if possible.*

He instantly replied that he owned a two story building on east 34th street (47) for which he had been trying to obtain a rental of one thousand per month. So he said "Why don't you boys move in? You can have the use of it." Then he had a better idea to the effect he would lease the building to the Foundation for a year at $1,000 a month and then make a donation of $12,000 to the Foundation with which to pay the rent, thereby making his gift deductible on his income tax. The papers for all this are being drawn right now, so I suppose the deal will go through.

The building is a "wow"! Each floor measures one hundred feet by twenty five, and ditto for the basement and the roof on which the brethren can sun themselves. There is even a small Italian garden in the rear. Since the largest contribution to date has been $250.00 I imagine that Friend Charles' contribution will cause the local philanthropists to raise their sights a little bit, in fact I seem to see such indications already.

I am much pleased with our office here at 30 Vesey Street. Lots of light and air — besides it overlooks a churchyard; recalcitrant drunks can take their choice of tombstone designs right from our windows.

We are getting swell reports from Los Angeles, San Francisco, Kansas City, Philadelphia, Washington, Richmond and Houston. If you know people in any of these places, let's have their names.

If we ever get over being broke, Lois and I will be out. We shall probably come anyway, within a few weeks I hope.

Affectionately,

After Bill and Lois were evicted from their Clinton Street home, they moved some fifty times in two years. They finally settled in their Bedford Hills home, which they lovingly called Stepping Stones. In April 1940 Dr. Bob wrote Bill another letter in which he seemed concerned about Bill's living circumstances.

Dear Bill,

Glad to hear from you again. Began to think that my letters to you, (two) one to Munsey and one to William Street, had both miscarried. Am much pleased that you have the new quarters and that they are so commodious and well located. I surely hope also that the budget can be taken care of. Have had two short notes from Chipman with enclosures but have heard nothing outside of that. Let me know about today's meeting shortly if anything of interest occurs. . . .

I still feel very strongly the less paid the better about anything of financial interest out here to anyone outside of myself. I hope very much, Bill, you will accede to my wishes in this respect at least for the present. . . . Perhaps you think I'm a bit fanatical on this subject. Maybe I am. We enjoy our new meeting place very much indeed. It seems just perfect for our purpose. Have had a couple of new boys from Toledo State Hospital (nut factory); this institution seems to have contacted us lately. Most of the boys are very nice. Where are you living now? I surely hope your material needs are being provided for; we shall be delighted to see you and Lois whenever you can come. The latch key to 855 [855 Ardmore Avenue, home of Bob and Anne Smith] *is always out for you.*

Throughout these letters, Dr. Bob seems very concerned about the financial well-being of both Bill and himself. His mention of the notes from "Chipman" with enclosures indicates that he had begun receiving at least some money as a result of the Rockefeller dinner.

After studying the communications between Dr. Bob and Bill and having knowledge of the economic times, I find it truly amazing that AA ever survived the pioneering time. Bill often called it "Providence" — it would be difficult to call it anything else. Everything seemed stacked against them, and still they persevered and kept their focus on helping other alcoholics.

chapter nine

Bill Speaks about AA's Future

IT WAS A TRADITION THAT BILL W. spoke numerous times at each of the AA International Conventions. This pattern started in 1950 with AA's First International Convention in Cleveland. He made a major speech, lasting over an hour, at each of these conventions and multiple shorter speeches. The only deviation was his last appearance at the Thirty-fifth Anniversary International Convention in Miami just months before he passed away from emphysema on January 21, 1971. He was so ill that he was barely able to make an appearance at all, and it had been announced that he would not attend.

After his partner, Dr. Bob, died in 1950, Bill became very determined to withdraw himself from his leadership role in AA. He knew it was time for AA to stand on its own, and it was his responsibility to turn the leadership over to the fellowship. This process began with the formation of the General Service Conference, which met as a trial for the first time in April 1951. By the time 1955 rolled around, the conference was fully established and Bill was ready to step down.

At the 1955 International Convention in St. Louis, Bill declared that AA had "come of age." He gave three historic speeches in St. Louis entitled "How We Learned to Recover,"

"How We Learned to Stay Together," and "How We Learned
to Serve." In the AA book *Alcoholics Anonymous Comes of Age*,
Bill shared parts of these speeches. The following was taken
directly from the original recording of "How We Learned to
Stay Together." Bill talks about the beginnings of AA and his
confidence in the future.

Well folks, hi! We're in a gay mood tonight and we certainly have
got a right to be. We are together, we know we're going to stay
together, we are at peace with each other, and we are at peace
with all those in the world around us. Why shouldn't we be gay?

So many troubles are behind us. Our destiny, praise God,
seems secure. It was not always this way. It was one thing for a
few alcoholics to get well. But this problem of living and working
together — that was quite something else. It was a very uncertain
time that we were looking upon from the windows of Dr. Bob's
living room when we first realized that alcoholics could get well.
But could we hang together? When the world around us — full of
more normal people — was being torn apart, could we carry this
message? Could we function? No man knew.

Our friends, the psychiatrists, have said with some cause,
"Why the explosive neurotic content of this society is just a mess.
It would be blown into smithereens." Well, when drunk we knew
we could be blown to smithereens, but now that we were sober,
yet subject to dry benders, emotional jags, would that rip us
apart? Speaking of this explosiveness when drunk, I'll have you
know that our chairman over here is called "Icky the Dynamite
Man." You see Icky is an expert on explosives, on demolition. I
think he was in the rear of the Russian retreat, blowing up bridges
during the world war. And he says that everybody but him came
home in a basket.

Well, when he got home, he started to apply his trade again
and I guess he fell under that same error that a poor fella in
London did here the other day. He appeared before the magistrate;
he'd been picked up stiff drunk. The bottle he had was empty.
The magistrate said, "Did you drink it all?"

"Oh, yes."

"But why did you drink it all?"

"Well," he said, "because I lost the cork." Well, it must have been one of those days that Icky lost the cork. He was commissioned to blow up a certain pier in Houston harbor and Icky blew up the wrong pier.

So the great question in the early days was this. Would we blow up or would we stay together? Would the grace of God that we already enjoyed be sufficient to hold in check the kinds of things that were driving wedges all throughout the modern world? That was a terrific question.

Well, this meeting here is a testament that we have held together. However, pioneering in AA hasn't stopped. I hope it never will. And while we feel very secure here today, there are places out on the AA front, in distant lands, on faraway beachheads where they are going through all the pains and worries of our pioneering times.

For example, the office in New York got a letter the other day and it was written by a Jesuit priest who was out in an isolated outpost somewhere in India. And he told a remarkable story. It seems that in that place there was a certain Hindu. The Hindu was a schoolteacher. The Hindu owned a cow. The Hindu had a plot of ground. He had a wife who was stone deaf and he had a sister who, like himself, also drank like a fish.

His salary as a teacher was about fifty cents a day. That's why they had to have the cow. The Jesuit had translated our Twelve Steps and lo-and-behold, this Hindu, in spite of his poverty, in spite of the deaf wife, in spite of the domineering and drunken sister, was staying sober.

I'll bet that lone Hindu out there is feeling the same worries that Dr. Bob and I felt in our living room. He is probably asking himself, "Can I hang together myself? Can I carry this message? Will we be able to form a group?" Yes, he's asking himself those questions. And he will soon be in communication with our office. And we'll try to send him assurance to that distant outpost, where pioneering is still going on.

I'm kind of old-fashioned. I still call Thailand, Siam. I guess the Siamese twins made a great impression on me when I was a kid. Anyhow, another letter came in almost the same day from a Presbyterian minister out there on another pioneering front. And he said, "You know, for a long time I've been trying to get an AA group started among the Thais out here and we've had a wonderful break. A highly educated one, speaking fluent English, has come along. He's been a really desperate case. And desperately wants to get well. He's very fluent in English.

"I'd like more of the AA literature. He's devoured it. He's been sober a good spell. And he wants to translate our entire literature into Siamese. And we're already at work starting groups. Can you give us a hand?" Well, of course, we're going to give them a hand — those pioneers out there.

And then he went on to add one thing more; a very thrilling thing it really is. He said, "You know we took the Twelve Steps over to the largest Buddhist monastery in this province and we got hold of the padre that's the head of it and he looked over the Twelve Steps and he said, 'Why these are fine, these are fine. It so happens that our particular branch of Buddhism doesn't understand God just as you do. It might be a little more acceptable if you inserted the word *good* in the Steps instead of God. But nevertheless, you define, in those Steps, it's *God as you understand Him*. Yes, these Steps will be accepted by Buddhists around here.'"

Well, what does this all mean? It means that almost surely there are going to be many AA groups in India, and in Siam, and in every place where alcoholics dwell in their caves. Maybe they aren't sure out there, but we're sure here, aren't we? Why, things that would have scared us to death years ago can give us a laugh. We can be gay now about our fears and our troubles of the old days. Speaking about these fears, a cute story turned up down in the office.

It seems that AA got its real start in Tokyo. Naturally, it started among the American drunks there and it spread out to the Japanese and there got to be quite a Japanese contingent, I am told. And we heard very good reports of them — when all of a sudden a Japanese appeared in the office.

Dr. Bob and Bill W. Speak

And he turned out to be the butler of a poor little rich boy down on Long Island. And both he and the poor little rich boy were terrific drunks and they'd both been in AA together, you know, a couple of years. And the Jap had heard that his fellows in Japan had groups and he'd begun to write them to get the inside track. And he came in, in great alarm. And he said, "You know terrible things are going on over there in Japan. Why," he said, "do you know that they have two kinds of AA there?" He said, "Of course they've got the Twelve Steps, just as we have them here. But," he said, "there is another AA leader there who now has eighteen steps. And for those eighteen steps he's charging 100 yen."

Now that sort of heresy, years ago, would have scared us to death. Today, it's only a laugh. We know they'll soon be infiltrated. We know that the fellow who means well and does badly will mend his ways. For this is a quest for survival — where sometimes the good is the enemy of the best. And nothing but the best can do the trick.

Well, I might go on with a fantasy lasting for hours about AA out on its distant reaches — its pioneering front. Do you know that there is a communication nightly that passes over here from tankers in the Atlantic to the Pacific by radio — AA members on each? Do you know of good ol' Captain "S" on the Standard Oil tanker, plying all through the world ports leaving AA literature, going ashore, looking up bartenders, asking for prospects? A group is just now starting in Florence, Italy, because an AA sailor comes ashore and gets a prospect off a bartender. Oh, the starts of these AA groups are very improbable seemingly.

But it has become literally true that where two or three of us are gathered together in His name, there will a group be. In fact, there doesn't have to be three. There's a wonderful story about that AA group way up toward Point Barrow, in Alaska. Maybe it's part fantasy, I don't know. I think there's some substance to it.

The story runs this way. A couple of prospectors go out, get themselves in a cabin. They got a case of scotch. The weather turned bitter, 50 below. They got so drunk they let the fire go out — a most perilous thing. Finally, one of them came to just in time; rekindled the fire and while prowling around outside he saw an empty oil drum with some water in it, frozen; brought the drum in and when she thawed out, there in the bottom was an AA book. One of the drunks sobered up. And the legend has it that he was the founder of one of our farthest north groups. Probably the one in which we now have so many Eskimos.

I'm told that in Alaska those farthest north groups are in communication by radio every day with an AA group that's on the North End of the Greenland Ice Cap, among the fellas up there on that air base. And so it goes — fantastically, miraculously, all over the world.

Dropping back now to some of the foreign groups that are in their adolescence, having severe growing pains, which they know they'll overcome. Oh, a lot of these come to mind. I think of the mining engineer who some years ago went to London. And he met up with the greens grocer. Today London is sprawling with groups. And they met such resistance in Britain, that at one time only the *Financial Chronicle* would publish an advertisement about AA, for fear this was a fraud.

I think of the tavern owner from Philadelphia who, with his wife, decided to go on a vacation to Ireland. When they got to Dublin, they said, "The dickens with the vacation. Let's start an AA group."

So they go to the local asylum, one endowed by "author Swift," and they find there their first man, and then a few more. And everybody knows Sackville who has written hundreds of us in all parts of the world. He's called the "Honorable Secretary." Abroad they're called Honorable Secretaries, not here.

Well, so it goes. In Australia years ago, the office began to get letters from a psychiatrist in a mental institution and a priest. And they'd got hold of some AA literature; and pretty much entirely by mail that whole development started. And Australia today is literally crawling with AAs, with the warmest public expression.

That's a long way from where Dr. Bob and I sat in the living room, our eyes turned toward the future. At that moment, in the fall of 1937, there were no Twelve Steps. But we had the essence of them and the word-of-mouth program — that little formula that Ebby dished out to me. There wasn't any AA book. We had grown very, very slowly and painfully.

And the next terrific development, following the publication of the AA book, was the immense commotion at Cleveland, Ohio. A few Clevelanders had been coming to the Akron meetings. And suddenly the *Cleveland Plain Dealer,* bless them, decided to run a series of pieces about Alcoholics Anonymous. And I guess the fellow who wrote them must have been a kindred spirit. And they ran ten of those in a row, right in a box, alongside, in the middle of the editorial page — ten smashing pieces about this society.

And every other day, an editorial would appear. Never before or since has there been such a terrific promotion. Hundreds and hundreds of telephone calls we received. The hospitals overflowed. And a group that had been only twenty mushroomed into several hundred within a matter of months. People were tossed into hospitals. Somebody visited them. They were handed the book. They went to one meeting and then that newcomer, he was an expert.

Up to this moment we had supposed that none but the very spiritual and experienced elders could administer this oath. But they found in Cleveland, that the almost-new man could make the essential identification and get his brother on his way. So we knew in the fall of 1939 that we could reach ties.[48]

In Toronto in July 1965, Bill W. gave what could easily be considered his greatest speech. He addressed the audience with a talk largely about humility and responsibility. He also presented to the members gathered there some of AA's most important business for the future. Although he spoke briefly at the 1970 Miami International Convention, it was in Toronto that Bill gave his last major talk to the worldwide fellowship. Because of the historical significance of this speech, I have decided to include it in its entirety.

Dear friends: With true magnificence and superb clarity, Bern [Bernard Smith, former chairman of the AA General Service Board] has portrayed the realities of our responsibility to the future. And he has been restating to us those eternal verities that gather around love, which are the substance of our aspirations. In effect, he has said, "Without humility, there can be no genuine responsibility. And lacking humility and responsibility, there can be no outgoing love freely given."

So it is well, that together here in this world convention, we have been pondering the subject of our future responsibilities. Since these cover a rather wide range, I think that my comments . . . could be best packaged up for you were I to paraphrase an article recently done, which some of you have seen in the *Grapevine*. So as a starter, dear folks, here goes.

17 "In AA's Thirtieth Year, Responsibility Is Our Theme," so it was titled. On the occasion of this, our thirtieth anniversary, it is ever so fitting that our keynote is AA responsibility. All of us have been thinking of those three decades of AA life that are now history. Stirred by gratitude quite beyond expression, we here give thanks to God, whose grace has made it possible for us to achieve that quality of responsibility which has brought our fellowship into its present state of well-being and worldwide reach.

As you and I look back over the years, we are quite unable to conceive of more than a mere fraction of what God has wrought among us. None of us can imagine the awful sum of the suffering that was once ours, nor the aggregate of the misery that has been the lot of those near and dear. Then, too, who can begin to understand the mysterious nature of our transforming spiritual experiences, those gifts of God that have opened to us of AA, a new world of being and doing and living.

Indeed, our blessings have been quite beyond any human comprehension. Here in Toronto, we see countless new faces. Many from distant lands are heard to speak in other tongues. We are dramatically reminded that the sun never sets upon this fellowship, that three hundred fifty thousand of us have recovered from our malady, that we have everywhere begun to transcend all those once formidable barriers of race, creed, and nationality.

Dr. Bob and Bill W. Speak

This new assurance that so many of us have been able to meet our responsibility for sobriety, for growth, and for effectiveness in the troubled world where we live, has filled us with the deepest satisfaction and joy.

Yet as a people who have always learned the hard way, we certainly do not congratulate ourselves. Instead, we perceive all these new assets to be God's gifts which have only, in part, been matched by an increased willingness on our part to find and to do His will for us. Then, too, we have well recalled how the painful desolation of our illness actually drove us to what was our first responsible decision, our first responsible act in years, that of joining AA. We remember how alcoholism had lashed us to such a point of collapse that we became willing to do whatever was necessary to get well, for indeed, it was a matter of life or death. Thus goaded on, we finally did join the fellowship and there we had our first glimpse of its quite new world of understanding and loving concern.

Presently, we took a look at AA's Twelve Steps for recovery. Yet, it must be admitted that some of us promptly forgot ten of them, as possibly not needed. At first, we bought only the concept that we were alcoholics, that attendance at meetings and a helping hand to the newcomers would be sufficient to solve our booze problem and, no doubt, all problems.

Indeed, some of us began to look with approval on the insidious old cliché which says that "drinking is but a good man's fall." Once off the grog, life should become, we thought, as pleasant as a bowl of cherries. So at first, we simply warmed our hands at the AA fire and all seemed well.

Then by slow degrees, certain dissatisfactions set in. Perhaps our own group was not so wonderful as we had first supposed, maybe there was some rock throwing at a scandal, or perhaps a distressing row. Who would become the group's next chairman? Then, too, we found that there were people we simply could not like, and we worshipped the ones we did admire, who often failed to give us the attention that we really deserved.

Even back at home we would have to get a shot once the pink cloud had passed over the household. Things sometimes seemed just as bad as ever; the old wounds simply wouldn't heal at all. Though visibly impressed with our sobriety, the bank, nevertheless, demanded to know when we were going to pay up. Our boss, likewise, requested in firm tones that we "get with it." At this point, each of us looked up at his sponsor and regaled him with these unexpected woes.

Those various resentments, anxieties, and depressions were definitely caused, we claim, either by our unfortunate circumstances or by the inconsiderate behavior of other people. Greatly to our consternation, our sponsors didn't seem in the least impressed. We can remember how many of them said, "Why don't we sit down and take a good, hard look at all of AA's Twelve Steps. Maybe you have been missing a great deal; in fact, perhaps you have been missing just about everything."

This was the point at which we began to take our own inventories and not the other fellow's. As we got into the swing of self-examination, we began to discover what our real responsibilities toward ourselves and toward those about us actually were. At first, this was a mighty tough assignment, but it did by degrees get easier.

Next, we commenced to make restitution to those we had harmed, grudgingly at first, then more willingly. Little by little it got through to us that genuine progress, spiritual or material, consisted in finding out what our responsibilities actually were, then proceeding to do something about them. Gradually these activities began to pay off. We found we didn't always have to be driven by pain and discontent. Much more willingly we picked up the burdens of living and of growing.

Then, surprisingly, we began to discover that full acceptance of any clear-cut responsibility nearly always made for true happiness and peace of mind. Moreover, these durable satisfactions were often redoubled when we realized that our now better quality of willingness made it possible, in meditation, to find and to do God's will. At last we joyfully knew that, at least most of the time, we really wanted a life of willing responsibility. Such was the course of our spiritual enfoldment, our pilgrim's progress if you'd like.

As it has been with each of us, so has it been with each group and with AA as a whole. For example, I have seen our society timid and fearful, angry and prideful, apathetic and indifferent. But just as often, I have seen these negatives fade as the lessons of group experience were at last learned and applied. Let me recall some instances of this.

In AA's early day, we were so timid; we felt we ought to be a real secret society. We shunned publicity because we still labored under the stigma of alcohol. Also, because we thought that publicity might overwhelm us by an influx, now mark this, of so-called "undesirable people."

When angered by criticism from within or without, we most often found ourselves far better at dishing out our own punches than taking the other fellow's. Sometimes we did boast that AA is the know-all and do-all of alcoholism, thus alienating our friends.

Shuddering at the awful perils of group wealth, we often did convert this fear into a marvelous alibi for failing to meet our trivial service expenses. And this, despite the fact, that these vital activities were indispensable to carrying AA's message into the world about us. Sometimes by poor sponsorship, or none at all, we did fail the needs of newly arrived sufferers.

Then at great turning points in AA history, our fellowship has in anger, or sheer indifference, at first backed away from what should have been clear-cut responsibilities. On a few occasions, disastrous results were barely avoided. A few very-old-timers can still recall the book *Alcoholics Anonymous* might never have been published because some in those days had vowed, "We do not need it." While others shrank from the hazards of preparing that absolutely essential text.

Ten years later we made a great outcry, some of us, against a formation of the General Service Conference of AA — that always-needed body of delegates which permanently links our society with its trustees and our active world services. For several years, we had held a belief that no such linkage could possibly be created. Many thought that any attempt at such a project would ruin us. It was commonly believed that we didn't even have sense to run a clubhouse. In consequence, this crucial undertaking nearly fell by the wayside from the sheer weight of indifference or maybe heavy attack and little faith.

Nevertheless, in God's good time, our spiritual assets did come to well exceed even these most serious liabilities. Today, recovery goes forward on a vast scale. The practice of the Twelve Traditions has amazingly cemented our unity. Our Intergroup associations and World Service Conference have made possible a widespread dissemination of our message at home and abroad.

Each time, it has been the same story. Our pains and our necessities have at first called us to a reluctant responsibility. But in these later years it is simply great to report that willingness and confident faith have more and more permeated our whole society, despite so much happy transcendence of the difficulties of yesterday. We do, nevertheless, deeply realize that our negative traits are still very much with us, and always will be.

Hence, our great and our continuous responsibility should be that of taking repeated fearless inventories of our defects as we go along—the better to undertake their mending. Therefore, here at Toronto, we are constantly asking ourselves, "What sort of heritage are we now leaving to all those generations of AA that will, in the future, people our society? Is the legacy that we shall bequeath them as good as we can possibly make it? While there is yet time, what can we still do that may multiply our assets and decrease our liabilities?

Now when I try to make such a survey of our society today, I hope none will regard me as one who presumes himself the righteous elder, who would admonish or exhort his followers. As I now inventory AA's shortcomings, please be assured that I too am taking my own. Well do I know that my errors of yesterday have left their mark, still have their effect; that my shortcomings of today and of tomorrow could likewise compromise AA's future. So then, let us together, take a hard look at the more important areas in the life of our fellowship, where the challenge for improvement will always be with us.

Our first concern should be for those sufferers of alcoholism that we are still unable to reach. Let us humbly recollect that throughout the world of today, there are some twenty million alcoholics, five million situated in the United States alone. These unbelievable numbers are, of course, in all stages of the sickness. Some cannot be reached because they are not ill enough, others because they are already hurt too much. Many suffer mental and emotional complications that seem to foreclose their recovery chances.

However, it would, I think, be conservative to estimate that at any particular time, there are perhaps four million alcoholics throughout the world who are able, ready, and willing to get well if only they knew how. Clearly, all these sick people need to know what their malady is, then to realize that they are so afflicted. Being so made ready, they then need to be brought within our reach, or indeed, within the reach of any other agency of rehabilitation. And this, by every resource of public information and word of mouth, can tell them exactly what steps they may take to find their road to recovery.

When we remember that in thirty years of AA existence we have reached but a small fraction of those four million we might have been able to help at any time, we commence to get an idea of the immensity of our future task, and of the vast responsibility with which we will always be charged. These arresting facts point straight to our next responsibility, a loving sponsorship of each alcoholic man and woman who comes among us asking for help. The concern and the care with which individually and collectively we do this can make all the difference to them. Again, I say the difference between life or death. Indeed this particular activity is the greatest expression of gratitude that we can ever make for what we ourselves have so freely received.

Perhaps a million alcoholics have taken a good look at AA during the last thirty years. Should we not then soberly ask ourselves, "What became of those six hundred thousand and more of fellow sufferers who did not stay with us? How much and how often did we fail all these?" This makes it most clear that in no

circumstances should we feel Alcoholics Anonymous to be the
know-all and do-all of alcoholism.

Right here in Canada and the U.S. alone, we have perhaps one
hundred agencies engaged in research, alcohol education, rehabilitation. Research has already come up with significant and helpful
findings and I'm certain the researchers are going to do far more.
Those engaged in education are telling the world that alcoholism is
an illness, that a great deal can now be done about it. Surely all of
these coworkers can make our own efforts ever more effective.

It is a known fact that such agencies in the United States and
Canada treat something like fifty thousand alcoholics each year.
To be sure, their approaches are often different from our own.
But why should this matter when many of these agencies are or
could be, in the future, entirely willing to cooperate with us of
AA and we with them? Too often, I think, we have deprecated,
even derided, these projects simply because we did not agree
with their methods. Had we not better now ask ourselves how
many alcoholics may have gone on drinking simply because we
have failed to go along in good spirit with some of these people?
Certainly, we must not believe that most alcoholics are going to
go mad or die simply because they did not come straight to AA in
the first place.

Now, let's look at this matter of criticism, especially the criticism of AA that is made in the world about us. For years, our
society has been amazingly exempt from those usual barbs that
are pitched at movements of any consequence, whether these
be social, political, medical, religious. For when this quite usual
thing does happen to us of AA, I think we are apt to register undue
shock, maybe anger, when people find fault.

Sometimes we have become so disturbed that we cannot even
benefit by constructive criticism. We are even less likely to be
good-natured about criticism; that it isn't so good; that it is criticism that is slanted or downright unfair. These are very natural
attitudes and I must say they are not widely general among us.
Yet, it is still a fact that many of us do so still react when we are
hit where we live.

However satisfying these brands of resentment to some of us personally, they make us no friends nor can they serve any useful purpose. Therefore, to react wisely and in good spirit to all criticism should be our constant aim.

Alcoholics Anonymous is not a religion nor is it a medical treatment nor does it profess expertise in respect of the unconscious motivations of human behavior. Sometimes I think these facts are too often overlooked by us. Here and there, we find members proclaiming AA to be a great new religion, excepting for purely sobering up assistance. We are also apt to underrate medical contributions to our welfare. Because the relatively new art of psychiatry does not yet sober great numbers of drunks, we are prone to discount the values of that profession.

When we take such unrealistic and negative attitudes we are, of course, forgetting that we AAs owe our very existence to medicine and to religion. In all our cardinal principles and attitudes, AA has made a misuse of these great resources. It is chiefly our friends in these fields who first gave us the principles that enable each of us to live and to grow today. Therefore, the credit of these vital contributors to our welfare should stand very high among us. True enough, we drunks did put AA together. Yet, its basic components were supplied to us by friends. Here especially, our maxim should be "Let's be friendly with those friends."

18 Next let us recall it is a historical fact that almost every group of men and women tends to become more dogmatic. As time passes, their beliefs and their practices harden, sometimes to the point of freezing. Up to a point, this is a natural process, not all of it bad. Certainly people must rally the call of their convictions. We of AA are in consequence no exceptions. Obviously, too, we should have the right to voice our convictions. This is good principle. This is good dogma; but dogma also has its liability. Simply because we have convictions that work well for us as of now, it becomes quite easy to assume that we have all of the truth. Whenever this sort of prideful arrogance develops, we become aggressive. We demand agreement with us. We play God. This is very bad dogma, indeed. For us of AA, it could someday become especially destructive.

For example, newcomers are approaching us at the rate of tens of thousands yearly. They represent nearly every belief and attitude imaginable. We have atheists and agnostics, people of many races, cultures, religions. Now, we of AA are supposed to be bound together in a kinship of common suffering. Hence, there must be full individual liberty to believe in any creed, in any principle, in any treatment. Surely these are liberties to be remembered by us.

Therefore never let us pressure people with our individual or even with our collective views. Instead, let us accord to each other that respect and love which is truly the due of every human being as he tries to make his way towards the light. Let us always try to be inclusive rather than exclusive. Let us forever remember that every alcoholic among us is a member of AA for so long as he or she so declares.

Some of our obvious perils will always gather around money, around controversies within and without, and about that ever-present human temptation to scramble for personal prestige and power. Our world of today is shattered by these untoward forces. So let us remember that as alcoholics we have been even more subject to these forms of destruction than other peoples. Thank God, we do have, and I trust to continue to have, a tremendous awareness of our responsibility for improvement in respect of these allurements. Our very survival and effectiveness will always depend on such an awareness.

However, the unreasoning fear of such evils should never deceive us into absurd rationalization when with lively debate a forthright action becomes a clear necessity. For fear of the ogres of prestige, or personal power, we should not weakly fail to endow our leaders in service with our full trust and a suitable authorization to act for us. Yes, prudence is a great virtue but timid indecision is often the greatest of vices. This is because no fellowship can exist or even prosper if it be leaderless.

So let us of AA never sidestep needed changes. Certainly we shall have to discriminate between change for the worse and change for the better. This is prudence, but once the need becomes apparent to the group or to AA as a whole, it has long since been shown that we cannot stand still or look back.

We have seen that the essence of all growth is found in the willingness to change for the better. This, followed by an unremitting effort to shoulder whatever responsibility is required of us. In conclusion, it is reasonable to say that we of AA have thus far been able in most areas of our lives together to make substantial gains both in willingness and capability for the acceptance and discharge of our obligation — something that this great gathering does well symbolize and demonstrate.

As we look forth into the future, we clearly see that these sterling attributes are the keys to that progress which God intends us to make as we move towards his appointed destiny. To these observations just made toward our growth in stature and in responsibility, I would now like to add a deeply important postscript.

As you and I stand at this turning point in history, I wish to pose to you the crucial question that besets every human society when its originators vanish from the scene. For us of AA, the precise question is this: Who will be the world's leaders of Alcoholics Anonymous in the years ahead?

About one half of my AA life has been devoted to World Service matters — services whose operation can today account for perhaps one half of our present membership, and much of our global unity. In consequence, the construction, the operation, the permanent maintenance of this chief world agency for carrying AA's message has been a chief interest of mine for more than twenty-five years. To make as sure as we can of a continuance of this vital work, there has always been implicit in our situation the difficult question of who will comprise primary world leaders of the AA fellowship in time to come.

For a long while there has been, of course, no doubt that our future top leadership will have to be chosen from our more important body of World Services, our trustees — the trustee members of the General Service Board. Most certainly, we cannot remain leaderless at the apex of our society.

In World Service matters it is, therefore, something for logic and something for necessity that our trustees will have to constitute the personal world leadership of AA's future. There is no other choice. Certain of this much, one might suppose that this serious question of AA's future leadership had already been settled. Yet, strangely enough, it has not been settled. Few AAs yet realize the gravity of the dilemma in which we who have been deeply concerned with this problem have found ourselves over the last ten years.

Happily, I now speak to you in no alarm because I believe that this question can soon be sensibly and responsibly resolved. Our dilemma of indecision has been as follows: as most of you know, AA's General Service Board includes two classes of trustee members — the non-alcoholic trustees and the AA trustees. As matters stand today, our non-alcoholic friends occupy a majority position on our board, this by majority of one.

Just as importantly, our non-alcoholics friends still tradition- ally supply the board with its chief officers: the treasurer and the chairman. Because of this unique setup devised in our infancy, the AA trustees of the board have remained in the minority. Hence, theirs has been a secondary responsibility in the leadership and conduct of world affairs.

Surely this arrangement is not today consistent with our pres- ent concepts of full AA responsibility in AA matters. From this brief portrayal, I trust that everyone here tonight can clearly see that our non-alcoholic trustees and officers are still cast in the actual role of primary leadership — not only of AA's World Service Board, but conceivably of AA as a whole over the years to come.

Against this background, our long unresolved leadership responsibility can therefore be summed up as follows: "Has the time yet arrived when our AA trustees should be majority of the service board, thereby becoming, in fact, the primary lead- ers of our fellowship throughout the world?" Still the question is, "Should AA's future world leadership be primarily of alcoholics or non-alcoholic friends?" It gives me the greatest of happiness and a relief to report to you that we may soon be able to arrive at a solu- tion of this serious issue.

About a year ago now, our non-alcoholic trustees came to a definite conclusion that the time has certainly arrived for the AA trustees of our board to shoulder the primary position of responsibility. Led by our well-loved chairman Dr. Jack [Dr. Jack Norris], these friends then took the initiatives in the preparation of a detailed plan for the transference of this great trust, a transference from themselves to us of AA.

At last April's General Service Conference, Dr. Jack presented this trustees' plan to our assembled delegates asking for a year's study and then for a vote at the 1966 conference. The delegates were also advised that nearly all the board alcoholics and AAs alike hope for its adoption. Dr. Jack's presentation will always be a magnificent highlight in my own life.

So it seemed right that I now conclude my part in this meeting by sharing with you the substance of this major undertaking and those comments which I ventured to make upon it on that most outstanding and memorable occasion. At the risk of a little overlap and repetition to you, I did speak to the 1965 conference delegates as follows.

Dear members, speaking on behalf of AA's Board of Trustees, our devoted friend and Chairman Dr. Jack has called upon us to face a far-reaching responsibility. Future AA historians will no doubt record this occasion as the major turning point in the enfoldment of our well-loved fellowship. This is because we are now to reconsider, and perhaps to recast the whole nature and composition of AA's future leadership. As we meditate upon this long unresolved problem, it would be well to recall that in the affairs of new societies, and of nations, the determination of their ultimate leadership has always been a matter of crucial importance.

This is the teaching of all human history. Dr. Jack has specifically requested us of Alcoholics Anonymous at the level of Board of the Trustees to assume the primary role in the conduct of world affairs. He has presented the detailed program for achieving this, a plan almost unanimously recommended by his fellow trustees. Should we adopt this new concept in 1966? The chief responsibility for the guidance of world affairs would then be shifted from the non-alcoholics of our present board to the alcoholic trustees of the newly recast board.

Our recast board would then be composed of fourteen AA trustees and seven non-alcoholic trustees. Seven of the AA members would be chosen from suitable areas of the U. S. and Canada, on the basis of their AA leadership qualifications. The remaining seven would be selected on the basis of their several high standards of business, professional, and administrative skills.

This would add up to a balanced board of twenty-one members in which the AAs would function in a majority of two to one. That would compare with our present board of ten non-alcoholics and nine AAs. The chief pulse of the new board would be open to its AA members at any time such a change might seem desirable; and for practical reasons alone the improved balance between these three classes of trustees should commend itself to us all.

However, the trustees plan as outlined by Dr. Jack has far greater implications than mere practicality. It carries deep spiritual values. It is the call to the highest of AA's responsibilities. In effect, it is a declaration that AA has now evolved to such a point of stability and competence that it should no longer need to function under what has been, since 1938, the symbol of protective custody by non-alcoholic friends.

As you know, the present structure was created long ago in the time when AA had but three groups and only forty members. It is worth pausing here to recall why our service board was originally so constituted. For us of AA the year 1938 was one of anguished uncertainty. There was no proof that alcoholics could stay sober indefinitely. Nor was there convincing evidence that we had the emotional stability to look after ourselves even though sober. Besides, we had no public standing. People did not know that we existed.

Then, too, how many distant AA groups would think of sending money contributions to a board of trustees composed wholly of New York alcoholics. This, dear friends, was the climate of fear and indecision that darkly overcast us in that early time.

Nevertheless, it had already become clear that our infant society would have to head up somewhere. At the top of our growing pyramid of membership, there was need to be erected a beacon light whose illumination might carry AA's message on the far reaches to those who still suffered alcoholism. Lest one day its radiance be snubbed out by drinking relapses and irresponsibility, we felt, in those days, that we dare not tend this lighthouse all by ourselves.

Some kind of certain protection we thought we had to have, but what kind of protection? The answer that we proposed in 1938 is now history. We asked carefully chosen non-alcoholic friends to become a majority of the trusteeship. We agreed to make this status legal. We stipulated that there should always be a non-alcoholic chairman and likewise a treasurer; frankly admitting that AA would have to have such a protectorate, we did somberly estimate that should every one of the AA trustees get drunk, our board could, nevertheless, continue to function by reason of its non-alcoholic members.

Happily we can now smile at these excessive fears and elaborate precautions. During the last twenty-seven years, only two AA trustees have been waylaid by alcohol.

Meanwhile, our message has been carried worldwide most effectively indeed. Half of our present membership, much of our unity has been due in large measure to the efforts of the AA World Service, on the Board of Trustees in the General Service Office, and more lately in the General Service Conference.

Of course, we service workers have witnessed severe emotional storms, but none more serious than those which affect most other societies. But in every single instance, these disturbances have been successfully overcome by the immense spirit of dedication that has always characterized every level of our worldwide effort. The record speaks for itself. Today we know that we need not fear alcoholism nor excessive emotional instability.

Now let us look back over the years and inquire what has been the value of our non-alcoholic friends all this while. Without hesitation, I can tell you that their value has been quite beyond any reckoning. Only God himself could add up their score.

Bill Speaks about AA's Future

Therefore, I deeply hope a sizable contingent of these friends will continue to remain with us, just as a new plan provides.

In the days when AA was unknown it was the non-alcoholic trustees who held up our hands before the whole world. They supplied us with ideas that are now a part of the working structure of headquarters. They cheerfully and voluntarily spent hours on end working side by side with us — sometimes among the grubbiest of the details. They gave freely of their professional and financial wisdom. Sometimes they helpfully mediated our difficulties. In the early years, especially, their presence in strength on our board was quite able to command the full confidence and respect of far-away AA groups. Meanwhile, they could assure the world around us of AA's worth. These are the unusual services which indeed they still render.

Then, too, these are the men who stood fast during that exciting though perilous time between 1940 and '50 when AA's unity and its collective responsibility were put to the acid test; a time when the Twelve Traditions were being forged out of the painful lessons of that experience. Having myself been a constant resident of AA's house of World Service for more than a quarter century, no one could better understand what these devoted friends meant to us. To gratefully set my testimony of their magnificent contributions on the record of this meeting is something for the deepest and most enduring of satisfactions.

Nor could any expression of our gratitude be complete unless I were to tell you of a certainly indispensable contribution that was once made to AA's welfare by a non-alcoholic friend and trustee. I speak of our one-time chairman, our beloved Bern Smith. During the most serious crisis that our fellowship has ever known, it was Bern who persuaded us to meet and to shoulder our clear and rightful obligations.

As individuals, it must be confessed that we AAs have never been overzealous to meet great responsibilities. We were driven to AA on the lash of alcohol. Arrived in AA, we were confronted with the Twelve Steps and Twelve Traditions. We proceeded to adopt these principles in a rather piecemeal fashion. But as time went by, the conformity began to improve. We commenced to practice these principles because we knew them to be right for us. Nonetheless, it was a very long time before many of us could come to the point where we would accept our heavy obligations with full and joyful willingness.

It has also been observable that like other people, we AAs are apt to resist any proposal for great change especially when all seems to be going well. Often enough, these reluctances have been based upon our fears. But sometimes they have represented a genuine prudence. This latter quality of conservatism has occasionally prevented ill-considered or hasty judgments upon important matters. What has been true of us as individuals has necessarily been true of AA as a whole. There was heavy opposition to the creation of world trusteeship in '38; to the book Alcoholics Anonymous in '39.

I still tremble when I recall the truly fierce resistance that rose in 1946 when our General Service Conference of Alcoholics Anonymous was first proposed. It was then seriously believed by a large majority of AA that the temptations and risks of such a complex venture as this would be too much for us. However, we may now thank God we finally did face and accept those vital and clear-cut responsibilities. Nevertheless, on every one of these occasions we found that we had to be strongly persuaded of the absolute need for change. There had to be manifest at those times a solid core of constructive and convincing personal leadership.

This is exactly what our remarkable friend, Bern, gave to us when in 1950 after several years of great heat but little light we had failed to arrive at a decision to form that General Service Conference. It was his personal leadership that saved the day for AA. Let me briefly background that statement.

By 1946, certain facts of AA life were becoming visible. Our trusteeship, then called the Alcoholic Foundation, was becoming more and more isolated as our groups fanned out over the globe. Indeed, the only linkage between our board and all these thousands of members really consisted of a few tireless AA gals at the General Service Office along with Dr. Bob and me.

*The trustees themselves had become virtually unknown. Dr.
Bob had fallen ill, perhaps fatally. Our linkage was, therefore, very
perishable and far too thin. Hence, some of us felt it imperative
that our Board of Trustees should be directly related without delay
to AA as a whole. There was still another reason. A majority of our
groups had already declared that they would no longer live under
the absolute protection and management of their local founders
and old-timers, no matter how well loved these were.*

*For better or worse, our groups had begun to make the deci-
sion to look after themselves. This was the AA revolution which
led to the writing of Tradition Two; whose principles of AA function provide that the group conscience shall be the final authority
for active services and that trusted servants named by the groups
shall act on their behalf. Certainly, our long isolated board members were trusted servants. But it was nevertheless true that the
trustees had no direct connection with the group conscience nor
were they directly accountable to it. It was therefore becoming
evident that we at New York were still operating as a protectorate,
something that had by then become obsolete — quite inconsistent
with the provisions in spirit of Tradition Two.*

*Consequently, it was proposed to assemble the General
Service Conference of delegates that might squarely meet these
deficiencies. As news of this project got into circulation, resistance
began to mount. The more the conference was urged, the more
the opposition dug in. Many AAs were deeply frightened. They
well imagined themselves engulfed in a wave of prestige seek-
ing, shabby politics, financial troubles, and all the rest of it. Under
such conditions many fine AA members were quite unable to see
the urgent need for this radical change. Observing their protests,
most of our board naturally concluded that AAs most emphatically
did not want such a conference.*

*Then too I'm afraid that the growing impasse was made still
worse by my own incessant bulldozing of this conference issue.
Then came Bern Smith on the scene with matchless diplomacy
and tact. He began to point out that the actual risk of the conference venture was, in his belief, far less than the risk of doing*

nothing at all — a policy which he thought would in the future result in a collapse or certainly a grievous impairment of AA at its very heart of service. He deeply felt that we must not risk such a debacle at headquarters, a calamity from which we might never wholly recover.

He also continued to remind us that self-direction was the very first responsibility of every democratic society, such as ours had in Tradition Two already claimed it was. As we all know, these views of Bern's were finally accepted. I shall never forget that wonderful day in his office when the trustees committee on structures recommended immediate creation of the General Service Conference of Alcoholics Anonymous. To our friend Bern, we therefore owe that we sit in this gathering of that General Service Conference today. Certainly, this story has deep and clear relevance to that all-important matter of AA's future leadership.

The question that is again before us, and one which has been ten years under debate, now is ever so evident that Dr. Jack has been performing us a similar service, a service of unique importance, one like Bern in the earlier time. To him and to his fellow trustees, we of Alcoholics Anonymous, therefore, owe a similar tribute. It is greatly due to Dr. Jack's wise and patient leadership in this time of change that we have the trustees' plan before us — a plan which, if we adopt it, will mark our last basic step in the evolution of AA's World Service Structure.

Most assuredly I hardly need say that I do endorse the trustees' plan. Its enfoldment in this General Service Conference meeting is one of the most inspiring and heartwarming events of my entire AA life.

Finally, let us reflect together upon the high spiritual contents of this all-important project. As we know, all AA progress can be reckoned in terms of just two words: humility and responsibility. Our entire spiritual development can be actually measured by the degree of our adherence to these magnificent standards: ever-deepening humility accompanied by an ever-greater willingness to accept and to act upon obligations. These are truly our touchstones for all growth in the life of the spirit. They hold up to us the *very essence of right being, and right doing. For it is by them that we are able to find and to do God's will.*

19 *Let us therefore consider the spiritual gifts which our friends, the non-alcoholics, have today offered for AA's future welfare. They have offered to reduce their numbers by three; still a board majority holding its chief posts. Our non-alcoholics, all these years, have been cast in the role of guardians — a responsibility that they have never really been called upon to meet. Therefore, this old-time symbol of protection long since became almost meaning-less. Our friends recognize this; therefore, their new trustees' plan provides that the non-alcoholics would, in the future, act in the minority, thus becoming our associates. In making this humble offer, they have called upon us of AA to assume the highest of responsibilities — the guidance under God of our own life as a fellowship.*

If then, this is their demonstration of humility, what is going to be our demonstration of responsibility? As to a family just coming of age, they have in substance told us the world of the future stretches before you. And you are well prepared. Go out into it fearing nothing. Our faith in you is confident. Indeed, it is very strong.

As you of AA move onward toward your destiny, may you always remember that God, in His wisdom, has granted you three precious graces: freedom from a deadly affliction, a life experi-ence that enables you to carry that priceless freedom to others, and a vision ever-widening of God's reality and of his love. May we of Alcoholics Anonymous remain ever worthy of these three gifts of grace, and especially of the supreme responsibilities that are now ours for so long as a bountiful God may wish our society to endure.[49]

epilogue

The Rest of the Story

I REMEMBER HEARING PAUL HARVEY on the radio when I was growing up. Paul would capture his audience with a descriptive and often inspiring story; then he would pause, usually for a commercial break, and return to conclude with the statement, "And now . . . the rest of the story."

In the preparation of this book, I scoured through nearly one hundred recordings of Bill W. and several of Dr. Bob and other pioneering AA members. I soon realized that there was no way for me to reduce AA's seventy-seven-year history into a book of several hundred pages. So I was faced with the dilemma of what to include and what to exclude.

My initial thoughts were to include only those pieces of AA history that were not generally known or written about. "Let's do this book differently!" I thought. This idea was at first exciting, but then I realized that most of AA's history had been told by both Dr. Bob and Bill many times over. Not only did they share the story of AA's beginnings, but also the same story has been shared by hundreds of AA members through the years.

I carefully listened to many versions of the "same story" looking for that special talk that had that magic — you know, the one that was just right! Again, I found myself attempting to qualify or judge comments being shared as part of someone else's story. I suppose it would be like listening to a certain speaker and concluding that "the message" just wasn't there — then later, talking with someone who found the message to be "life-changing."

As with many things in life, it's often a matter perception: Is the glass half full or half empty? More and more throughout the writing of this book, I became aware of the fact that each person reading or listening would likely be affected differently by the same passage. One might be stirred while another was completely unaffected. And furthermore, what doesn't interest someone today might be exactly what they are needing or wanting tomorrow.

For these reasons, in presenting the various talks and topics in the book, I made every effort to remove my opinions, feelings, and emotions, simply wishing to offer an eclectic array of AA history, gathered from different points along the seventy-seven-year timeline.

In the end, my goal was simply to let Dr. Bob and Bill "speak" and, along with some of the other founders, tell this miraculous story in their own words. These people were the architects of a movement that started with two drunks sitting together in a library on Mother's Day 1935 exchanging their stories with one another. They found comfort and hope in each other. Little did they know that they would carry that message to a troubled world.

Dr. Bob and Bill both had visions of what AA might one day be. They wanted the fellowship to be available to all future generations, and they desired to see others recover through the principles they adopted in their early sobriety. This is why they published *Alcoholics Anonymous* and developed the AA Twelve Steps and Twelve Traditions, and the "Three Legacies" of AA (Recovery, Unity, and Service). They worked tirelessly to develop and protect AA by creating a General Service Board that would take over that responsibility when they could no longer serve.

Bill occasionally commented on what slender threads the fellowship hung on. So many different times he, Dr. Bob, and the other early members could have given up and allowed AA to collapse. The challenges that they faced were seemingly insurmountable. Early difficulties including their own sobriety (Dr. Bob was the first one to have a slip) and a lack of success when carrying the message to others would have been reason enough to give up.

Most people would have probably retreated, but these men seem to have been handpicked by Divine Providence to construct this "Fellowship of the Spirit" that has been the archway by which millions of men and women have entered into a new life, a life of freedom, joy, and happiness.

They acknowledged that "unity and the common welfare" were paramount for AA's survival. Imagine looking down from space upon the millions and millions of people worldwide who are currently involved in the recovery community joining hands in a circle. It would be impossible to distinguish any particular individual trait: age, sex, religion, economic or social background, political views, or length of sobriety. Each person would look the same—one link in the chain that binds them together in unity.

Perhaps today if Dr. Bob and Bill W. were to look down upon the fellowship they would say, "Good job. Keep carrying the message to the still-suffering alcoholic. Give freely what has been freely given you, and enjoy the rest of the story."

appendix A

Bill W.'s Interview with Mike Wallace

AA'S TRADITION ELEVEN READS, "Our public relations policy is based on attraction rather than promotion; we need always maintain personal anonymity at the level of press, radio, and films."[50]

During Bill W.'s life he was presented with many opportunities to get into the public eye. He turned down most of these opportunities and repeatedly declined any personal recognition, including the front page of *Time* magazine. His example of personal sacrifice was a testament to his practice of genuine humility and dedication to AA principles. He turned down multiple awards, including three different honorary degrees, one from Yale University.

Bill limited his public appearances because of the tradition of anonymity, but he also recognized that as AA's leader he couldn't simply hide away. The most widely used media in the 1950s was the radio and Bill had the opportunity in 1956 to appear on several radio broadcasts. He requested that his anonymity be respected and that he be referred to only as Bill.

The following transcription is of a radio interview between Mike Wallace, his cohost Virginia Graham, and Bill W. on NBC's Weekday Radio, recorded in 1956. The following key indicates who's speaking: MW = Mike Wallace, VG = Virginia Graham, and BW = Bill W.

This interview seems to capture the spirit of the AA message perfectly and has what can be considered significant historical content. Therefore, I have elected to share the entire interview here.

VG: *Alcoholics Anonymous is an organization that is helping 150,000 men and women throughout the world achieve continuing sobriety.*

MW: *Founded twenty-one years ago the one purpose, the one objective of AA is to help alcoholics recover from their illness. Bill, welcome to* Weekday *and tell us, first of all, if you will, sir, what kind of a problem specifically is alcoholism?*

BW: *First let me thank you deeply for having us AAs on the air. Well, it's certainly a public problem. There's supposed to be about four million alcoholics in the country. If you know a drinker, you certainly know it's a social problem. In the early days the doctors used to think that there was nothing inherited, certainly you don't inherit a craving for grog. We do notice in AA, though, that certain families have a great many alcoholics and it has been suggested that very likely they get emotionally bummed up and made neurotic and therefore laid wide open to alcohol. Not because it is strictly inherited; it's more an environmental thing.*

VG: *Of course, you see the parents drinking a lot and people around the home and you fall into the habit and may not have the capacity for evaluation.*

MW: *But you would think that somebody in the family where somebody older is an alcoholic, the youngster would see the bad effect of the alcohol and thus stay away from it.*

BW: *You're exactly right, they often do. They go to an extreme of great hatred of drinking of all sorts on one side or later they themselves fall victim. It usually runs to extremes; they either reform or get drunk.*

VG: *Don't you think, Bill, that in most instances it's the case of someone having a great disappointment or a circumstance that forces them into this?*

BW: *Well, in my own case there was childhood inferiority. I was big, gawky; kids could push me around. And that developed a tremendous power drive to be "number one chap." You see I had to be leader of everything, and then when frustrated I would become depressed. This pattern in me developed before there was any alcoholism.*

Well, then I found, on my first drink indeed, during WWI that it cured the social inferiority. People came near to me; I drew near to them. It was a solace; it wasn't just a mere relaxation. I had begun to try to cure what you might say is a neurotic pattern. And that is the case with a great many alcoholics, but generalization is dangerous. Some alcoholics are simply addicts; and there are a great many types. And as I say, this is for the doctors rather than for AA. I can only speculate, a little, on my own case.

MW: *Now, my understanding is that when you go to a party, for instance, you can never have just one drink; you, yourself, an alcoholic.*

BW: *No, no more than a diabetic can have one spoon of sugar. And probably he's a lot more sane about the sugar than we are about the alcohol. Because we not only have the physical sensitivity, there is this terrible obsession or drive to drink which has to be released. And if you take one drink it triggers the whole business.*

VG: *You know, Bill, it's a funny thing how you acquire a pattern. Now I had a similar experience as a youngster. Now I saw someone, a very beautiful woman, get drunk when I was a child and you know I have never had a drink. My problem was going to parties with people who do drink and I have my own little beverage called "water on the rocks," which I drink. Perhaps my resentment is, as you say, as radical as the person who over-drinks.*

MW: Now just a second, Virginia! What do you mean you've never had a drink? We had a champagne party right here in this studio.

VG: Now listen to this; I'm nailed to the cross. I had one thimble-full of champagne (Wallace interrupts jokingly saying that she was flying) and I was flying out to get rid of it.

MW: How, Bill, can you get a person to face up to the fact that he is an alcoholic?

BW: In the early days of AA they only faced up because they laid on their backs and couldn't move and it was do or die. In that period we dealt with "last gasp" cases only. But in recent years more and more people are recognizing that they have the symptoms; this compulsion to drink when they shouldn't be drinking. This terrible hangover business and it's just as though your doctor came to you and said, "I don't like the looks of this growth." And he takes a culture and he says, "Well, it's very small, but very malignant; it's cancer."

So likewise, a lot of people are recognizing these symptoms and coming in much earlier. We're getting a lot of young people, a lot of people not in any great trouble.

MW: What is an alcoholic? How do you know if you are an alcoholic?

BW: Well, I would say that the easiest definition hangs around the word "control." If when you should control your drinking, and you wish to control it, and you still do not, that is one of the great warning symptoms. It is this compulsive desire to drink against your will and against your interests.

If I go to a Legion convention where everybody is supposed to get tight and I get tight, it's meaningless. On the other hand, if I have a business appointment and I don't meet it because I'm tight or I come in there and ball it up, I may still be a long way from the poorhouse, I may not have been in the hospital yet, the family may still be together; but that's the telltale thing. The lack of control when there should be control; when you're trying to control and it wont.

VG: When one drink is too much and fourteen isn't enough.

BW: That's about the score.

VG: Now in the area of activity with AA about how many "cures" would you say have been effected?

BW: Well, I'll correct you. There are recoveries, but we think we have 150,000. Easily, the movement is spread now into seventy countries and U.S. possessions. It goes on pyramiding; we're in a tremendous period of growth just now, one alcoholic carrying the message to another.

VG: Of course, you're not an organization in the full sense of the word; how does a family — let's say somebody wants to discuss a problem with a member of their family who, by the way, is not receptive to AA. Now this to me is a big problem of bringing the offender to a meeting because they have to come voluntarily, don't they?

BW: Nowadays doctors and clergymen both are very, very helpful in laying the groundwork for AA. They can raise the bottom and hit the chap with it and most always it's best to try the doctor first. If the doctor will say, "Look, you have the symptoms of this thing. We're not going to force you into AA; we know that that's no way. But why don't you go and inform yourself about this? Go to an AA meeting." Sometimes literature falls into their hands or it can be left around, but you cannot force people into AA. They have to be attracted to it somehow and they have to go strictly of their own interests.

MW: Now your plan is a twenty-four-hour plan as I understand it. I shouldn't say the entire plan is; would you explain what the twenty-four-hour plan is?

BW: That's one of our clichés which is becoming notable. It simply means that emotionally we do not live in the past or in the future; we try to live for today.

MW: Get through the next twenty-for hours.

BW: Let's go through the next twenty-four hours without a drink and that is the springboard that most people take off on *at the very beginning until they have a basic fundamental release so that the problem becomes non-existent. They go on this twenty-four-hour basis and the information is that we mustn't morbidly dwell on the past or daydream about the future. Let's live, "One day at a time."*

VG: I wonder if you would be kind enough to repeat for us the "Serenity Prayer" used by AA, Bill.

20

BW: God, grant us the serenity to accept the things we cannot change, courage to change the things we can, and wisdom to know the difference.

VG: Isn't that wonderful?

MW: It sure is, not just for AA. God, grant us the serenity to accept the things we cannot change, courage to change the things that we can, and the wisdom to know the difference.

VG: I think that the description of the prayer, as Bill said before: he said, "It's like a tent; it encompasses and covers all of us."

MW: Thank you so much, Bill, for being with us this morning.

BW: Again, our great thanks to you people.

VG: And God bless you in your work.

appendix B

Correspondence between Bill W. and Dr. Bob, Spring 1940

THE DINNER HOSTED BY JOHN D. ROCKEFELLER, JR., in February 1940 prompted the exchange of letters transcribed at the end of chapter 8. The letters themselves appear on the next four pages. On March 29 Bill W. wrote to Dr. Bob, recounting an offer of New York City real estate for use by the fledgling Alcoholics Anonymous organization — an indirect outcome of the "Union Club dinner." "The building is a 'wow'!" Bill enthused. Dr. Bob responded a few days later, on April 1. AA was growing quickly.

30 Vesey St.,
New York City.
March 29, 1940

Dear Smithy:

Little by little the results of the Union Club dinner are becoming apparent in several ways, not that the Foundation treasury is bulging as it still has only about three thousand dollars. Practically all of the gentlemen who attended the dinner, and quite a lot of those who did not, contributed. There was a large amount of enthusiastic comment and letter writing, but the amount of dough required seemed so small to the gentlemen that each contributed only a little. A little while ago I got a letter from Mr. Rockefeller expressing great pleasure over the impression the A.A. created at the dinner. Also commending our unselfish and effort, etc.. There is a meeting next Monday to consider ways and means to finish up the job, so I have no doubt that we shall arrive in time at whatever place we are supposed to be going. The number one philanthropist, however, at this writing is Mr. Charles Noyes.

You remember talking with him about his brother the night of the dinner. The brother came to town the other day and Charles set out a really good meal for the three of us at his town house. During the course of the dinner he said we ought to have more local publicity and mentioned a series of articles in the New York World similar to the Plain Dealer series. I remarked that before doing anything like that we had to have a local headquarters of some seating capacity with office and club arrangements if possible. He instantly replied that he owned a two story building on east 34th street (47) for which he had been trying to obtain a rental of one thousand per month. So he said "Why don't you boys move in? You can have the use of it." Then he had a better idea to the effect he would lease the building to The Foundation for a year at $1,000 a month and then make a donation of $12,000 to the Foundation with which to pay the rent. Thereby making his gift deductible on his income tax. The papers for all this are being drawn right now, so I suppose the deal will go through.

The building is a wow! Each floor measures one hundred feet by twenty five, and ditto for the basement and the roof on which the brethren can sun themselves. There is even a small Italian garden in the rear. Since the largest contribution to date has been $250.00 I imagine that Friend Charles contribution will cause the local philanthopists to raise their sights a little bit, in fact I seem to see such indications already.

I am much pleased with our office here at 30 Vesey Street. Lots of light and air -- besides it overlooks a churchyard, recalcitrant drunks can take their choice of tombstone designs right from our windows.

We are getting swell reports from Los Angeles, San Francisco, Kansas City, Philadelphia, Washington, Richmond and Houston. If you know people in any of these places, lets have their names.

If we ever get over being broke, Lois and I will be out. We shall probably come anyway, within a few weeks I hope.

Affectionately,

Dr. Bob and Bill W. Speak

DR. R. H. SMITH, M.D.

HOURS:
2 TO 4 P.M.

SURGEON
810 SECOND NATIONAL BUILDING
AKRON, OHIO

PHONES:
OFFICE: HEMLOCK 8523
RESIDENCE: UNIVERSITY 2436

Dear Bill :-

Glad to hear from you again. Begin't think
that my letters to you (2) one to Ruensey + one to
William St. had both miscarried. Am much
pleased that you have the new quarters and that
they are so commodious + well located. I
surely hope also that the budget can be
taken care of also. Have had two short
notes from Shipman with enclosures but have
heard nothing outside of that. Let me know
about todays meeting shortly if anything of
interest occurs. The Snyder setup about
which I was so much perturbed is about the
same. Dorothy spent one week end with us
+ I hope we were able to cheer up the poor
soul. She was also down yesterday but the

Correspondence between Bill W. and Dr. Bob, Spring 1940

Roland Jones + were down to Wooster & spent the PM. there with the Jones family. They are really very fine people. Betty has not been well of late. We seem to be moving at about the usual clip. I have been about half on the sick list myself for the past few weeks with a few days in bed but think I am beginning to emerge from the woods now tho am a bit weak yet. I still feel very strongly the less said the better about anything of financial interest out here to anyone outside of myself. I hope very much, Bill, you will accede to my wishes in this respect at least for the present + remember that Ruth + Dorothy are very close. Perhaps you think I am a bit fanatical on this subject. Maybe I am. We enjoy our new meeting place very much indeed. It seems just perfect for

over

...us purpose. Has had a couple of new boys from the Toledo State Hosp. (nut factory) which institution seems to have adopted us lately. Most of the boys are very nice. Where are you living now? I surely hope your material needs are being provided for. We shall be delighted to see your & Lois whenever you can come. The latch keen to 855 is always out for you. Make it as soon as you can. For my dearest to the little woman.

affecly
Bob
Mrs Frank Curtis
Forest Farms
Newport

Correspondence between Bill W. and Dr. Bob, Spring 1940

appendix C

A Personal Exchange between Dr. Bob and Bill W. by Wire

In June of 1947, the Smiths recorded a personal message to the Wilsons on a "wire recorder" — a novel technology for the home — and sent it to them. Visiting the Smiths at the time was George H., an early member and close friend of both Bill and Bob. In the recording, Dr. Bob also mentions Archie T., the founder of AA in Detroit, for whom he served as sponsor.

🔊 *Bob: According to [Archie T.], the infamous [George H.] has*
21 *descended on the Smiths for a short time, which is really an unexpected pleasure. We are both confined to the house yet, but have hopes of getting out in circulation before too long. I regret, and Anne also, that we can't come to Bedford Hills for a little recuperative period right now. But if you'll give us a rain check, maybe we'll show up next fall or winter. They tell us that we are doing very nicely, although I have discovered that surgery varies a good deal as to whether it's done on you or you do it on the other fellow. This changes the picture quite a bit. I think possibly my recent experience will make me a little kinder and more thoughtful towards those who are recipients of my handicraft. We at least*

can look forward to a nice chat with you, I hope in the early fall. And we appreciate the fact that you are willing to extend us the rain check.

Bill Wilson replied by recording his own message just a few days later.

Hello, Anne and Bob! Isn't this a great gadget we get to talk through? It was mighty good to hear from George how much better you both are! You have no idea how terrifically concerned so many of us have been. Now that the worst is over we can all now breathe better.

I have just been having a long talk with George about the state of AA affairs throughout the country. And he has sharpened up to me, as he as doubtless did to you, the tremendous necessity of getting some sort of council organized which can relate the foundation to the AA groups. I also went over the internal situation here with George, and on the whole he is inclined to think that the changes suggested in the reorganization plan are really necessary for us here in New York before we start the formation of a council.

We'd awfully much like to know if you won't come down to Bedford Hills sooner than the fall; but I suppose there's small use in begging you. You know, I still feel awkward and hard put to find words to talk into this microphone. As you see, I have a good deal of "mike fright" — even now I'm beginning to get more and more confused. In fact, my face is getting quite red. For you know, I'm not one who usually lacks words.

Lois and I hope that you both will surely get well and strong and that very fast. We think of you so very, very much, dear people, and look forward to the moment when we can see her — see you — I've still got the mike fright.

George H. then introduces Bill playing the violin for the Smiths, which closes out the recording.

Obituary Excerpts

Akron Beacon Journal
October 16, 1950

Dr. Robert Holbrook "Bob" Smith, co-founder of Alcoholics Anonymous, died of cancer, his physicians said today. . . . A physician and surgeon in Akron for 40 years, Dr. Smith was 71. . . . With a New York broker known as Bill W., Dr. Smith helped to found Alcoholics Anonymous here in June 1935. It grew to an organization of more than 100,000 members, with groups in such distant lands as Saudi-Arabia, England, Ireland, South Africa and most lately, among American GI's in Korea. . . . Dr. Smith and Bill W. together devised the program for what later became AA — combining the spiritual, psychological, and work with other alcoholics.

New York Times
January 26, 1971

William Griffith Wilson died late Sunday night and, with the announcement of his death, was revealed to have been the Bill W. who was a co-founder of Alcoholics Anonymous. . . .

[In 1934] he gained an introduction to Dr. Robert Holbrook Smith, a surgeon and fellow Vermonter who had vainly sought medical cures and religious help for his compulsive drinking.

Bill W. discussed with the doctor his former drinking pattern and his eventual release from compulsion.

"Bill was the first living human with whom I had ever talked who intelligently discussed my problem from actual experience," Dr. Bob, as he became known, said later. "He talked my language."

The new friends agreed to share with each other and with fellow alcoholics their experience, strength and hope. The society of Alcoholics Anonymous was born on June 10, 1935 — the day on which Dr. Bob downed his last drink and embraced the new program. . . .Mr. Wilson called Dr. Bob "the rock on which the A.A. is founded. Under his sponsorship, assisted briefly by myself, the first A.A. group in the world was born in Akron in June, 1935."

The Twelve Steps of Alcoholics Anonymous

1. We admitted we were powerless over alcohol—that our lives had become unmanageable.
2. Came to believe that a Power greater than ourselves could restore us to sanity.
3. Made a decision to turn our will and our lives over to the care of God *as we understood Him.*
4. Made a searching and fearless moral inventory of ourselves.
5. Admitted to God, to ourselves, and to another human being the exact nature of our wrongs.
6. Were entirely ready to have God remove all these defects of character.
7. Humbly asked Him to remove our shortcomings.
8. Made a list of all persons we had harmed, and became willing to make amends to them all.
9. Made direct amends to such people wherever possible, except when to do so would injure them or others.

10. Continued to take personal inventory and when we were wrong promptly admitted it.

11. Sought through prayer and meditation to improve our conscious contact with God *as we understood Him,* praying only for knowledge of His will for us and the power to carry that out.

12. Having had a spiritual awakening as the result of these steps, we tried to carry this message to alcoholics, and to practice these principles in all our affairs.

The Twelve Traditions of Alcoholics Anonymous

1. Our common welfare should come first; personal recovery depends upon A.A. unity.

2. For our group purpose there is but one ultimate authority — a loving God as He may express Himself in our group conscience. Our leaders are but trusted servants; they do not govern.

3. The only requirement for A.A. membership is a desire to stop drinking.

4. Each group should be autonomous except in matters affecting other groups or A.A. as a whole.

5. Each group has but one primary purpose — to carry its message to the alcoholic who still suffers.

6. An A.A. group ought never endorse, finance, or lend the A.A. name to any related facility or outside enterprise, lest problems of money, property, and prestige divert us from our primary purpose.

7. Every A.A. group ought to be fully self-supporting, declining outside contributions.

8. Alcoholics Anonymous should remain forever non-professional, but our service centers may employ special workers.

9. A.A., as such, ought never be organized; but we may create service boards or committees directly responsible to those they serve.

10. Alcoholics Anonymous has no opinion on outside issues; hence the A.A. name ought never be drawn into public controversy.

11. Our public relations policy is based on attraction rather than promotion; we need always maintain personal anonymity at the level of press, radio, and films.

12. Anonymity is the spiritual foundation of all our Traditions, ever reminding us to place principles before personalities.

Reprinted from *Alcoholics Anonymous,* 4th ed. (New York: Alcoholics Anonymous World Services, 2001), 562.

notes

Author's Note: *Many of the audio sources cited in this book are part of the Fitzpatrick Archive, a large collection of audio recordings, now in my possession, that trace the history of the Twelve Step movement. Digitization of the audio files is underway, bringing the voices of this legacy to a new generation. More information on the archive can be found at the Recovery Speakers website, www.recoveryspeakers.org. Another collection in my possession, known as the Recovery Speakers Research Library, consists of print resources related to Twelve Step history, such as letters, interview transcripts, conference records, and other historical documents.*

Introduction

1. Howard P., interview with author, Gilbert, AZ.

2. The Bronx cocktail ("da Bronx") is a gin-based drink that combines sweet and dry vermouth enlivened by a splash of orange juice. In the 1930s, it was in such demand at New York's Brass Rail in the Waldorf that the bar, under the tutelage of Johnny Solon, went through many cases of oranges a day.

3. Bill W., speech in Dallas, TX, June 1951.

Chapter 1

4. Excerpted from "Bill's Story" in *Alcoholics Anonymous,* 4th edition (New York: AA World Services, 2001), pp. 8–9.

5. Ibid., p. 12.

6. This passage is drawn from eight audio recordings of Ebby T. in the Fitzpatrick Archive, www.recoveryspeakers.org:

> Ebby T., AA meeting in Memphis, TN, September 14, 1958.
>
> Ebby T., Texas State Convention, Fort Worth, TX, June 11–13, 1954.
>
> Ebby T., Great Bend, KS, February 21, 1961.
>
> Ebby T., Davenport, IA, May 11, 1960.
>
> Ebby T., San Francisco, March 5, 1961.
>
> Ebby T., talk at AA meeting in Kansas City, MO.
>
> Ebby T., speaking from hotel room at the Twentieth Anniversary of Alcoholics Anonymous in St. Louis, July 1955.
>
> Ebby T., talk at AA International Convention, Long Beach, CA, July 1960.

7. Bill W., letter dated Dec. 1, 1961, archives at Stepping Stones, the historic home of Bill and Lois Wilson in Bedford Hills, New York.

8. Margaret McPike, letter dated March 26, 1966, Recovery Speakers Research Library.

Chapter 2

9. Bill W., speech in Chicago, February 1951. Fitzpatrick Archive, www.recoveryspeakers.org.

10. Excerpted from *Alcoholic Anonymous*, pp. 8–14.

11. Bill W., speech, AA International Doctors Conference, Indianapolis, 1966, Fitzpatrick Archive, www.recoveryspeakers.org.

12. John H. of Hilton Head, South Carolina, conversation with author, July 2010.

13. Bill W., speech in Atlanta, June 1951, Fitzpatrick Archive, www.recoveryspeakers.org.

14. Bill W., speech at his twentieth anniversary celebration, November 1954, New York City. Fitzpatrick Archive, www.recoveryspeakers.org.

15. Dr. Bob, speech in Detroit, December 1948 (his last major address). Fitzpatrick Archive, www.recoveryspeakers.org.

16. Bob S. Jr., speech in Kerrville, TX, 1986. Fitzpatrick Archive, www.recoveryspeakers.org.

17. Michael Fitzpatrick, *We Recovered Too: The Family Groups' Beginnings in the Pioneers' Own Words* (Center City, MN: Hazelden), 2011.

18. Bill W., speech at Nineteenth Founders Day, Akron, OH, June 1954. Fitzpatrick Archive, www.recoveryspeakers.org.

Chapter 4

19. Longtime AA member, historian, and author Tom W. of Odessa, TX, phone conversation with author, February 12, 2012.

20. Bill W, speech at Nineteenth Founders Day, Akron, OH, June 1954. Fitzpatrick Archive, www.recoveryspeakers.org.

21. Bob S. Jr., speech in Kerrville, TX, 1986. Fitzpatrick Archive, www.recoveryspeakers.org.

22. Eddie R., letter to Bill W., Alcoholics Anonymous World Services archives.

23. Excerpted from "He Sold Himself Short" in *Alcoholics Anonymous,* 4th ed. (New York: Alcoholics Anonymous World Services, 2001), pp. 262–263. Used with permission.

24. Clarence S. of St. Petersburg, FL (formerly of Cleveland, OH), speech at Top O Texas Roundup, Lake Brownwood, TX, October 14, 1960. Fitzpatrick Archive, www.recoveryspeakers.org.

25. Bill D. (AA number 3) of Akron, speech in Canton, OH, 1951. Fitzpatrick Archive, www.recoveryspeakers.org.

26. Speech by Bob S. Jr., Kerrville, TX, 1986

27. F.B.B. (an admirer of Anne S.), letter written in her memory, Recovery Speakers Research Library.

28. Tom W. of Odessa, TX, phone conversation with author, February 2012.

29. *Dr. Bob and the Good Oldtimers* (New York: Alcoholics Anonymous World Services, 1980), p. 125.

Chapter 5

30. Bill W., speech at AA's International Convention, Long Beach, CA, July 2–4, 1960. Fitzpatrick Archive, www.recoveryspeakers.org.

31. Bill W., talk at Sister Ignatia's Golden Jubilee Celebration, Akron, OH, June 20, 1965. Fitzpatrick Archive, www.recoveryspeakers.org.

32. William G. Borchert and Michael Fitzpatrick, *1000 Years of Sobriety* (Center City, MN: Hazelden), 2010.

33. "Started in 1946, the annual Lasker awards have been presented to individuals and groups which have made major contributions to public health efforts. This prestigious award is often compared to the Nobel Prize, and many of its laureates have received both honors. The presentation was made in San Francisco at the Opera House on October 30, 1951. Mr. Bernard Smith (nonalcoholic), former chairman of the Board of the Alcoholic Foundation (now the General Service Board), accepted the award on behalf of Alcoholics Anonymous." (Reported on Alcoholics Anonymous website, www.aa.org/lang/en/subpage.cfm?page=401.)

34. Bill W., speech in San Francisco, October 1951. Fitzpatrick Archive, www.recoveryspeakers.org.

35. Bill W., introduction of Sister Ignatia at AA's International Convention (first meeting), Long Beach, CA, July 2–4, 1960. Fitzpatrick Archive, www.recoveryspeakers.org.

36. Sister Ignatia, speech, AA's International Convention (first meeting), Long Beach, CA, July 2–4, 1960. Fitzpatrick Archive, www.recoveryspeakers.org.

37. Meeting chair, introduction of Sister Ignatia at AA's International Convention (second meeting), Long Beach, CA, July 2–4, 1960. Fitzpatrick Archive, www.recoveryspeakers.org.

38. Sister Ignatia, speech at AA's International Convention (second meeting), Long Beach, CA, July 2–4, 1960. Fitzpatrick Archive, www.recoveryspeakers.org.

Chapter 6

39. Dr. Bob's farewell speech, First International AA Convention, Cleveland, OH, July 27, 1950. Fitzpatrick Archive, www.recoveryspeakers.org.

40. Letter from Sigmund Freud to Wilhelm Fliess, Dec. 22, 1897, quoted in Rik Lose, *The Subject of Addiction: Psychoanalysis and the Administration of Enjoyment* (London: Karnac), p. 30.

41. Dr. Bob's farewell speech, Cleveland, OH, July 1950, Fitzpatrick Archive, www.recoveryspeakers.org.

42. Bob S. Jr., speech in Kerrville, TX, 1986. Fitzpatrick Archive, www.recoveryspeakers.org.

43. Dr. Bob, speech in Detroit, 1948 (his last major address). Fitzpatrick Archive, www.recoveryspeakers.org.

Chapter 7

44. Marty Mann went on to become the founder of the National Committee on Alcohol Education, later renamed the National Council on Alcoholism and Drug Dependence.

45. Bill W., speech to the Manhattan Group, New York City, December 1955. Fitzpatrick Archive, www.recoveryspeakers.org.

46. Ibid.

Chapter 8

47. *Alcoholics Anonymous Comes of Age* (New York: Alcoholics Anonymous World Services, 2010), p. 184.

48. Bill W., "How We Learned to Stay Together," speech at Twentieth Anniversary Celebration, AA International Convention, St. Louis, July 1955. Fitzpatrick Archive, www.recoveryspeakers.org.

49. Bill W., speech at AA's International Convention, Toronto, July 1965. Fitzpatrick Archive, www.recoveryspeakers.org.

Epilogue

50. *Twelve Steps and Twelve Traditions* (New York: Alcoholics Anonymous World Services, 1981), p. 180.

about the author

Michael Fitzpatrick is a leading historian and speaker in the field of alcoholism, specializing in the development of the Twelve Step movement. Author of *We Recovered Too: The Family Groups' Beginnings in the Pioneers' Own Words,* he is also coauthor of *1000 Years of Sobriety* (with William G. Borchert) and *Living the Twelve Traditions in Today's World: Principles Before Personalities* (with Mel B.). Mike owns what is possibly the largest audio archive related to the Twelve Step movement ever assembled, containing more than three thousand original reel-to-reel recordings of the voices of the men and women who pioneered the Twelve Step movement. Mike is in the process of digitizing these recordings, which are now being made available online at recoveryspeakers.org. Many of the transcripts in this book and recordings included in the accompanying CD and e-book are from this archive.

Mike lives in Chandler, Arizona, with his wife, Joy, and their three children. He and Joy work together to operate his business as a book broker and marketing consultant. Over the years Mike has written sales promotional pieces and training manuals for several major corporations.

He has traveled extensively throughout the United States and Canada as a guest speaker and sales leader, motivating and inspiring his audiences with both his humor and his inspirational message of hope. His message to sales organizations is "attitude is everything!"